# OUTSTANDING SHORT PLAYS

## VOLUME TWO

### Edited by CRAIG POSPISIL

★

★

DRAMATISTS
PLAY SERVICE
INC.

OUTSTANDING SHORT PLAYS: VOLUME TWO
Copyright © 2015, Dramatists Play Service, Inc.

All Rights Reserved

**SPECIAL NOTE**

Anyone receiving permission to produce any or all of the Plays in the volume OUTSTANDING SHORT PLAYS: VOLUME TWO is required to give credit to the Author as sole and exclusive Author of the Play(s) on the title page of all programs distributed in connection with performances of the Play(s) and in all instances in which the title(s) of the Play(s) appears for purposes of advertising, publicizing or otherwise exploiting the Play(s) and/or a production thereof. Please see your production license for font size and typeface requirements.

Be advised that there may be additional credits required in all programs and promotional material. Such language will be listed under the "Additional Billing" section of production licenses. It is the licensee's responsibility to ensure any and all required billing is included in the requisite places, per the terms of the license.

**SPECIAL NOTE ON SONGS AND RECORDINGS**

For performances of copyrighted songs, arrangements or recordings mentioned in these Plays, the permission of the copyright owner(s) must be obtained. Other songs, arrangements or recordings may be substituted provided permission from the copyright owner(s) of such songs, arrangements or recordings is obtained; or songs, arrangements or recordings in the public domain may be substituted.

# INTRODUCTION

The idea behind the first volume of OUTSTANDING SHORT PLAYS was simple. More than a few of our playwrights had one-acts that were too short to be published in their own Acting Editions but were certainly worth adding to our catalogue. The plays in that collection were both comedies and dramas; some were new, and others had been written some time ago. In fact, Christopher Durang wrote DISTRACTIONS when he was still in college.

So, I didn't have a theme in mind when I began to collect another group of short plays. I was just looking for good plays, on varied topics, and by both emerging and established authors. But after selecting the titles that make up this second volume of OUTSTANDING SHORT PLAYS, it strikes me that all of them are about navigating the tricky waters of relationships.

In some of these plays you'll find characters struggling to get their closest friends and family to understand some very basic truths, like in Amelia Roper's CAMBERWELL HOUSE, where a long friendship takes a dangerous turn, and in Harry Kondoleon's SELF-TORTURE AND STRENUOUS EXERCISE, where two couples wrestle with the conflicting desires in their twisted marriages.

In other plays, like David Riedy's SOMETHING FROM NOTHING, Aurin Squire's FREEFALLING, and David Ives' A SINGULAR KINDA GUY, you'll find the drama playing out in the characters' heads rather than in a more literal space — but the underlying struggle is one of understanding and trying to be understood.

The characters in Arlene Hutton's CLOSING COSTS and Rob Ackerman's YOU HAVE ARRIVED are just meeting. Both authors explore the way modern technology can help or hinder first dates, first meetings, and first impressions.

John Patrick Shanley's POISON, Aoise Stratford's THE CLOSET, and my play, THERE'S NO HERE HERE, are more stylized and fantastical than the others in the collection, featuring a powerful fortune-teller, living children's toys, and a long-dead American writer. At heart, however, these plays are about lost love.

I love short plays, and I think finding a good one is like finding a perfect gem. Reading the plays in this collection, I hope you will agree.

—Craig Pospisil
*March 2015*
*New York City*

# CONTENTS

# CAMBERWELL HOUSE

## BY AMELIA ROPER

# CHARACTERS

ANNIE, age 75.


# SETTING

The inside of Annie's apartment.
A faint smell of roses and old perfume.
One chair, something hard.
A table, or something like a table.
On the table, a small house.


# NOTES

The house is Camberwell House, a small apartment block where Annie, Olive, Mr. Wu, and Mr. Avery live.

Camberwell is an inner-city suburb of Melbourne, Australia. There is no need for accents. Enjoy the voice you have.

This is not a naturalistic monologue. This is a play with puppetry, or A/V, or whatever you do best. An ideal performance space might be a living room, and not a theatre at all.

CAMBERWELL HOUSE was first produced in Melbourne, Australia, in 2008. It was directed by the playwright.

# CAMBERWELL HOUSE

*An old woman sits alone.*

ANNIE.   Olive says she understood life the day she understood furniture.

It must have been when she was young, she didn't say.
We were talking on the stairs.

People talk on stairs.
            Not the sort of talk you need to clarify.
                        Not the sort of talk you need at all, really,

but,
well,

it's just good to know someone's there,
when you're seventy-five and on stairs.

*(Annie reaches into her purse and pulls out a small chair.)*

Olive says she ran into the kitchen,
running from a boy,
or called in by her mother.
Yes she must have been young, to have been called in by her mother,
although, her mother, but but oh, she must have been young to
have been running, yes, because it wasn't the war yet,
and suddenly,

chairs.

*(Annie reaches into her purse and pulls out three more chairs.)*

Olive says she ran into the kitchen, suddenly.
She saw her mother, her father, and a lady from the church.
She saw them sitting, and she saw the chairs they sat on,
and she saw the truth!

About furniture!

She saw that they did not sit down because chairs were there,
but that the chairs had been designed, built, and bought
out of a desire
         to sit

           down!

*(Annie drops the chairs into the windows, one chair in each apartment. The family of chairs become four individuals, living alone.)*

This discovery, like the best of discoveries, led to others.

*(Annie continues to pull furniture from her purse.)*

The table! The table had things on it! Things not bought to go on the table but the table bought for somewhere to put the things! Cupboards were the same, beds too. Cups and plates and even clothes-pegs. Good God! Was everything in her house in her house for a reason? Perhaps it was!

*(Annie shoves the rest of the furniture into the house.)*

Not that there weren't exceptions. Plates are plates, but her mother had some plates hanging on the wall. Why? Why is this something people do?

*(Annie holds up a small floral cushioned chair on the palm of her hand.)*

And her mother had a good chair where no one was allowed to sit. The good chair was in the good lounge where no one was allowed to go. Is this because they were bad? Or just not good enough?

So I think what Olive was trying to tell me, that day on the stairs, is that sometimes chairs are built to sit in. And sometimes plates are bought to eat off. And sometimes,
they're not.

Olive doesn't have very much furniture.
None of us do.

*(Annie holds up the good chair, admiring it.)*

But what she has she completely understands.

*(Annie shoves the good chair into Olive's window.)*

Olive lives here.

*(A light in Olive's window, a warm yellow light. Then a light in the next window.)*

Next to me. And of course we do! Of course we live up here!
If we didn't we wouldn't have been talking on the stairs!
Or if we were talking on the stairs,
              when our rooms are down there,

*(Annie points to bottom floor windows.)*

you might wonder why. You might even follow us,
if you were Mr. Avery you would follow us, you would write it down,
in a notebook.

      "Where are you going?
      What are you up to?"

Or if you were Mr. Wu,
learning his English from cassette tapes.
If you were Mr. Wu you might say,

      "My older sister is older than my older brother,
      and she has retired in excellent health."

It is his phrase for the day.
Mr. Wu lives here.

*(A light comes on in Mr. Wu's window. Mr. Wu lives below Annie; she smiles down at him. She drops a chair through Mr. Wu's window, trying to see in.)*

Mr. Wu says if I ever call out, he will save me.
He says even if I fall, suddenly, and don't call out he might still save me, he might still hear me, he says.

Mr. Wu wears very large earphones when he listens to his cassette tapes and he listens to them all day.

So.

We shall see.

*(A light in a far window flickers on, a colder color, a fluorescent.)*

Mr. Avery says Mr. Wu is a spy.
Mr. Avery lives here.

*(Annie points to the window, the one with the cold light.)*

Small man. War hero.
You might have seen him on your way up,
hiding behind a plant.

*(Annie throws a chair at Mr. Avery.)*

Olive says Mr. Avery is a poet.
And I say, "No he's not."
And Mr. Avery writes this down,
and Mr. Wu says,

> "My older sister is older than my older brother ... "

*(Annie is remembering something; what is it? It doesn't matter.)*

We've been friends for years and years, Olive and I.
Never miss a Christmas or birthday despite our finances.

I give her library books.

She has to return them three weeks later
but they are always beautifully wrapped and well chosen.
A little money goes a long way if you are careful.
I might live for years and years if I am careful.
Careful not to eat any of Olive's cooking!


My mother lived for years, and now I'm older than she ever was
and that's a strange thing, to be older than your own mother.

If there is a heaven, and if I go,
the twins will be five and eighteen.
My mother will be seventy.
My father, seventeen.

My Tom will be thirty-six.

And what will he think of me?
I will be the oldest, the matriarch.
Not because I was born first but because I died last which is a much
greater achievement, don't you think?

How old will Olive be?

Younger than me, I imagine.
She has trouble on the stairs.
We climb them together when we can.
And then we drink tea and eat biscuits.
As a reward.

For being so old.

Olive baked ginger nut biscuits this morning.
There is a plate of them on my front mat.
She knocked but

I pretended not to be in because

Olive

      is trying

          to

                    kill me.

I didn't want to believe it at first
but it does seem that way

unfortunately.

All my fault. Something we did when we were young. Something we
said when we were nurses together.

At twenty, being old seemed like the worst possible thing to happen
to a person! At twenty, being thirty seemed like the worst possible
thing to happen to a person. Second only to babies!

Before we knew worse things of course.
Before my brother left his legs in France.
Before, well,
this and that,

you know.

So Olive and I, we made an agreement.
If we were still alive at seventy-five we would,
well, we would,

          knock each other off!

We'd do it in secret and with as little pain as possible.
Whoever got in first, well!

Lucky
for the other!

Who could want to live past seventy-five!
I had an apartment near a woman who was seventy-five and you
never wanted to get stuck behind her on the stairs.

Hours

it took her.
More when it was cold.
                    Six flights!
            Not one, like here.
Six flights and now I think

Gosh!

A woman like that doing six flights a day! What a woman!
What a wonderful triumph against everything that hurts
when you are an old woman.

So many things.

Six flights.

Last August, when I was still seventy-four,
I remembered all this, and thank goodness I did!

So much life spent trying not to die you see,
I'd almost forgotten!

Olive remembered too,
but I told her
I didn't want any part in it.
We were young and foolish when we said it
and what did we know about life then?
We knew nothing at all!

*(Annie points to her audience.)*

Just like you now.

I still do the stairs quite well, thank you.
I've only fallen once and that was on Mr. Avery's cat
who was already dead no matter what he tells you.

I enjoy small things.
I like cinnamon on my toast.
I like remembering to turn my electric blanket on early.
I also quite like remembering to turn it off which I didn't last night
and that was unpleasant.

I will be more careful in future.

Olive likes things too.
Olive likes to do the same things most days
because
Olive's memory is going.

She doesn't remember that her husband is dead.
She doesn't remember that ginger nut biscuits hurt my teeth.
She doesn't remember that her youngest son left his
legs in Vietnam
and is shocked each time she sees him.


What is it with men leaving their legs all over the place?


Olive only remembers how things were.
The chairs you sit on
          and the ones you don't.

She remembers the agreement we made when we were twenty

But

she doesn't remember August
when I changed
my
mind.

Yes.
You see.

Now you understand.

A bit of a
mess, really.

A shame.
Olive is such fun.
Last week we had a sherry together on her mother's good chair.
We talked about the women in our book group
and why we don't like them.

Mr. Wu came rushing in and said

"There has been an earthquake and we must go far from here.
The dogs and the rabbits, they have already left,
how did they know?"

It was his phrase for the day.
He had a sherry too and we all sat very still,
knowing that

right then


all was well in the world,
and if we were quiet
it might stay that way

just
a
little
longer.

*(Annie sits.)*

But it didn't.
And the moment I got up to leave, she hit me with the frying pan.

Sometimes, when I think she is about to hit me, I ask Olive
if she remembers our little agreement.

        "Yes,"
she says,
        "That old thing. So long ago."
        "Yes,"
I say,
        "so long ago.
         I don't want any part of it now.
         I am happy.
         I want to be ninety."

And most days, when I tell her I want to be ninety, she says,

        "Oh"
and looks a little disappointed.

Once I told her as I was about to take a sip of tea.
She said,

        "Then you probably shouldn't
         drink that."

So don't eat the ginger nuts on your way out. Who knows what she
put in them. The quiche finished off Mr. Avery's cat. Died
on
        the
             stairs.

That was why I tripped over him.
Olive has fallen a few times now.

Not on cats
specifically, just,
you know,
as people do.
She has trouble on the stairs.
Sometimes she sits half way down,
waiting for me to come home.
On those days all she can do is cry and say,

"I wish I'd had a daughter to look after me." She'll say,
"What is an old woman meant to do all day?" She'll say,
"What is it I am meant to do all day?" She'll say,

"All the best things are gone."

I will visit Olive tomorrow.
I will tell her about the cat!
I will tell her how I left my electric blanket on
and dreamed of being lost in the desert.

I will take the ginger nut biscuits.

I will tell her I
                baked them
                        myself.

That I baked them
                for her.

She won't remember.

I'll do this
because
she doesn't have a daughter
to look after her.

She only has me.

And we,

we had
an agreement.


*(Perhaps the stage lights fade, leaving only the small lights in the small house, or something else entirely.)*

**End of Play**

# PROPERTY LIST

Purse
Small house with windows
Small furniture

# THE CLOSET

## BY AOISE STRATFORD

# CHARACTERS

BERNARD, a toy dinosaur.

BART SPONGE, a toy sponge.

TWINKLES, a toy.

# SETTING

A closet under the stairs. Set dressing can be minimal,
but it should portray a space used for storing the unwanted.

# NOTES

Running time: ten minutes.

On costuming: While elaborate character costumes would be great, this play should be very easy to produce and, consequently, costuming can be kept very simple. At a minimum, Bernard should wear purple, and he needs a tail, even if it's just a pair of stuffed pantyhose hanging out of the back of his pants. Twinkles should wear purple and carry a red bag. Bart Sponge should wear loose shorts and a tie. You get the idea.

On casting: Bernard and Bart are male, and they should be played by men; Bart is younger than Bernard. Twinkles can be played by a woman or a man of any age.

THE CLOSET was first produced by City Theatre in Miami, Florida, in 2006. It was directed by Stuart Meltzer. The cast was as follows:

BERNARD ............................................................ Ken Clement
BART SPONGE ...................................................... Joe Kimble
TWINKLES ...................................................... Antonio Amadeo

# THE CLOSET

*A closet. Piles of newspapers, discarded shoes, tennis racquets, etc. Bernard sits flicking idly through a copy of* Playboy, *his long purple dinosaur tail hanging out of the back of his overalls. Twinkles, a small, overstuffed purple toy holding a red handbag, is bouncing around, looking at his own feet, and giggling. A beat. The door to the closet opens and Bart Sponge is hurled inside. The door slams. Bart Sponge picks himself up and goes quickly to the door. It's locked. The sound of retreating footsteps.*

TWINKLES. *(Waving.)* Hello.

BART SPONGE. *(Calling through the door.)* Please! Mr. Peterson!

TWINKLES. Hello.

BART SPONGE. Kevin, are you out there? Hey! I'm in here.

TWINKLES. Hello.

BERNARD. Hey, you. Sponge. The Tubby is talking to you. Show some respect.

BART SPONGE. *(Rattling the door.)* Sorry. I … Oh, jeez, it won't open.

TWINKLES. *(Waving.)* Hello.

BART SPONGE. Okay. Hi.

TWINKLES. Hello.

BERNARD. He gets it already. He said hi. Now leave him alone. Christ on a crutch.

BART SPONGE. Do you know how to get out of here?

BERNARD. Out of the closet? Ha! That's a good one.

BART SPONGE. The … closet? *(A beat.)* Oh my … I can't stay here.

BERNARD. What's the matter? Don't you like what I've done with the place?

BART SPONGE. Well, it's okay, I guess, but … ah, about this door …

BERNARD.  Probably a little messy for a neat-freak like you. I tried to get on one of those TV makeover shows, you know, where those queer guys come in and bust up the place, give you new cushions, put a whole bunch of fucking candles everywhere and make you buy expensive hair gel and shit. No one would take me on. I guess closets ain't commercial. Still. It's not so bad. You get used to it.

BART SPONGE.  Right. Um … I'm sure that's true, but I don't think I'm supposed to be in here. There's been a mix-up.

BERNARD.  Oh really? What happened? You get mistaken for a mop or something?

BART SPONGE.  Well, I'm not quite sure. Mr. Peterson got back from a business trip late last night, and first thing this morning he came and grabbed me out of the toybox and … well, here I am. Kevin is very attached to me; if he doesn't know his dad put me in here he might worry.

BERNARD.  And then again, he might not. He never came looking for me.

BART SPONGE.  Oh. Well … I'm sure …

BERNARD.  Can't expect too much from the kid. He is only three. *(A long pause. Bart Sponge puts his ear to the door. Listens. Nothing.)* The sooner you forget about it, the sooner you get used to it. That weird Harry Potter kid spent years in a closet under the stairs.

BART SPONGE.  Years? Oh dear me. Have you been here long?

BERNARD.  You trying to pick me up?

BART SPONGE.  What?

BERNARD.  *(Lecherous.)* Come here often? *(A beat. Bart Sponge is quietly terrified.)* It was a joke.

TWINKLES.  Joke! Funny! *(Giggles inanely.)*

BART SPONGE.  Oh. *(Forces a laugh. Tries to open the door.)*

BERNARD.  Relax. Where's the fire? Kevin's probably on his way to daycare by now, so you may as well get comfy. What's your name, anyway?

BART SPONGE.  I'm Bart Sponge Round Trousers. Kevin's favorite toy.

BERNARD.  Pleased to meet you. I'm Bernard the dinosaur. Kevin's ex-favorite toy. And this here is Twinkles. He's a Tubby, whatever the hell that is.

TWINKLES.  Twinkles say hello!

BERNARD.  Jesus in jelly, what Kevin was thinking with that one, I'll never know.

BART SPONGE. Well, maybe when he was younger …

BERNARD. Yeah. Right. Kids these days outgrow that kinda shit in the womb. *(Takes a crumpled pack of American Spirits and offers one to Bart Sponge.)* Cigarette? They're the good ones. No chemicals. Don't want to set a bad example.

BART SPONGE. Ah, no thanks.

BERNARD. So. What are you in for?

BART SPONGE. I'm sorry?

BERNARD. The closet, Spongepants, what are you in for?

BART SPONGE. It's Bart. Bart Sponge. And I'm, well, like I said, I'm just in here temporarily.

BERNARD. Yeah, that's what I thought. Were you a Christmas present?

BART SPONGE. Yes. Santa brought me. I was the best thing under the tree, so I'm sure Kevin'll want to get me back. I've got moveable parts, look! *(Waving his arms and legs.)* And my pants come off too.

BERNARD. Hey! Keep those on! Shit, no wonder they canned you.

BART SPONGE. I'm not canned. I can't be. I'm Kevin's favorite.

BERNARD. Yeah, yeah. So you said. Look, kid, I hate to be the one to break it to you, but toys that go into the closet don't come out. So what did you do? It's less than a month after Christmas; it must have been something big.

BART SPONGE. I didn't do anything. I'm innocent.

BERNARD. No such thing, Spongehead. Come on, you can tell your Uncle Bernard.

BART SPONGE. I didn't do anything. Really.

BERNARD. Let me guess. Did you sneak into Kevin's sister's room and try to dress up in her Barbie's outfits?

BART SPONGE. No! Why on earth would I do that?

BERNARD. *(Gesturing crudely.)* You didn't get caught bending over that teddy, did ya?

BART SPONGE. What? Bending … what?

BERNARD. Well, it musta been something. I've never known Kevin to just get bored with a toy after only a few weeks … Even the tub-tub lasted a few months, and look at it. Wait! I got it! Weren't you in that Teach Kids Tolerance video! The one that Pro-Family Foundation dude said was corrupting kids and turning them all gay.

BART SPONGE. You heard about that video?

BERNARD. Sure; it was in the paper. Even the governor knows about it, and he doesn't know shit from cookie dough. *(Gets up and dances suggestively while singing a line or two from a disco tune. Twinkles bounces around, excited, trying to join in. Bart Sponge is appalled.)*

BART SPONGE. Oh, please, don't ... Do you mind my asking, which paper?

BERNARD. All of 'em, Bath Boy, you're famous. Mrs. Peterson keeps the recycling in here, so we get the *New York Times* and the *Examiner*, plus the *National Enquirer* if she's been to the supermarket.

BART SPONGE. You really think that's why Mr. Peterson put me in here? Because of a video?

BERNARD. You bet your big, round tush it is. Do you think he wants a little faggot like you playing with his precious son, Kevin? It was bad enough when you were just running around your fruity fucking palace in your tighty-fucking-whities and holding hands with that limp-dick pink thing ... /

BART SPONGE. Hey! You can't say that about my friend Patrick /

BERNARD. ... But then you had to go and get yourself associated with some leftie video promoting diversity awareness or some crap and send it out to schools all over the country. Face it, the conservatives are right: You're as camp as a row a' tents, as gay as Tuesday, as queer as a three-dollar bill. You ain't getting outta here any time soon. I might just be the best friend you got. *(Bart Sponge contemplates this a moment and runs to the door, pounding on it.)*

BART SPONGE. Kevin! I'm in here. Mr. Peterson, I'm sorry, let me out!

BERNARD. Relax. Do I look like I want to fuck you? *(Holds up the girlie magazine.)* Trust me; you're not my type. I'm more likely to stick it into Twinkles over there.

TWINKLES. *(Giggles.)* In. Out. In. Out!

BART SPONGE. *(Rattling the door.)* Help! Let me out! Let me oouuuttttt.

BERNARD. Do you have to make so much noise? *(Takes a step toward Bart Sponge. Bart Sponge turns on him, ready to fight.)*

BART SPONGE. Get away from me! If you try anything I'll ... I'll ...

BERNARD. Dude, get real. I'm a fucking plush and plastic toy. What am I going to do to you? Maul you to death with my felt teeth? Just give it up, will you?

BART SPONGE. I know karate!

BERNARD. I won't hurt you. I won't even make a pass at you.

BART SPONGE. *(Beat.)* Promise?

BERNARD. Cross my heart. Besides, it won't do you any good bashing on that door. Forget Kevin; the stink of scandal is on you now, my friend, and there ain't no going back from that. I should know. I was on TV once. All I did was clap my hands a lot and hug a few little boys. Big fucking deal. They let Wacko Jacko off, but not me, oh no. Look at that fucking thing, they said. Purple velvet is way too fucking gay, must drive a stick shift; take him away in the night while Kevin is sleeping and shove him down here in the dark. Forgotten. *(Beat.)* Look, I'm sorry if I came off a little gruff. I didn't mean to give you a hard time. I'm not that used to interacting with celebrities, and it's pretty hard to practice your social graces when you're living in a closet with someone like Twinkles. *(Beat.)* Truth is, I'm kinda lonely and I could use a friend. I gotta tell ya, I'm real glad you're here. The Tubby is driving me fucking nuts. *(Twinkles starts jumping in little circles and swinging his handbag.)*

BART SPONGE. I can imagine.

BERNARD. He's a little hard to converse with.

BART SPONGE. It's a he?

BERNARD. Well … in a manner of speaking.

BART SPONGE. Wow.

BERNARD. Yeah. You think you got problems.

BART SPONGE. So. What do we do now? If we can't open the door. What's the plan? Do we just wait for it all to blow over?

BERNARD. Not a lot of choice. Mrs. Peterson comes in once a week with the recycling. You could try to make a run for it then, but you won't get far on those legs, and chances are next time you'll be straight off to the trash can. If I were you, I'd try and keep a low profile. Hope for the best. *(Beat. Pats the floor next to him.)* Come on, take a load off. You may as well conserve your energy. *(They sit on the floor, side by side, beaten.)* So … just out of curiosity, Spongebutt, are you?

BART SPONGE. Gay?

BERNARD. Yeah.

BART SPONGE. I don't know … I'm a sponge.

BERNARD. Oh. *(Beat.)* Do you miss Kevin?

BART SPONGE. Yeah. He was nice to me. You?

BERNARD. Yeah. Not as much as the little guy does though. It's been really rough on him. *(Twinkles comes over to sit with them, sadly. Bernard gives him a hug.)*

TWINKLES. Miss Kevin. Twinkles miss Kevin too.

BART SPONGE. Well, we'll all just have to stick together. Toys belong with kids. That's the natural way of things, right? I mean, what else are we for? They'll see that sooner or later. Kevin will come to rescue us. Just you wait and see. *(The toys sit. Waiting. Lights slowly fade to black.)*

## End of Play

# PROPERTY LIST

Pack of American Spirit cigarettes
*Playboy* magazine

# SOUND EFFECTS

Retreating footsteps

# CLOSING COSTS

## BY ARLENE HUTTON

## CHARACTERS

ALICE

HARRIS

## SETTING

An empty loft apartment in SoHo, New York City.

*For Lori Wolter Hudson, with much thanks.*

## ACKNOWLEDGMENTS

Special thanks to Margot Avery, Seth Barrish, Lee Brock, Dana Brooke, Christine Cirker, Jenny Eakes, Kelli Lynn Harrison, Lori Wolter Hudson, Alice Jankell, Lou Liberatore, Dawn McGee, Pat McLaughlin, Bob McNamara, Jane Petrov, Porter Pickard, Craig Pospisil, Emory Van Cleve, FAB Women, and Ensemble Studio Theatre First Brew.

CLOSING COSTS premiered as part of Short Stuff VII at the Barrow Group (Seth Barrish and Lee Brock, Co-Artistic Directors) in New York City, on July 29, 2013. It was directed by Lori Wolter Hudson; the set design was by Caite Hevner; the lighting design was by Marika Kent; and the stage manager was Christine Lemme. The cast was as follows:

ALICE ............................................................. Tricia Alexandro
HARRIS ................................................................. Cayleb Long

# CLOSING COSTS

*Lights up on Alice, a nicely dressed real estate broker, and her new client, Harris, an attractive businessman around the same age. Harris has a handheld device — an iPad, smartphone, or whatever gizmo is the most up-to-the-minute technology for data entry. Harris focuses on his device ... until he doesn't. Alice talks quickly ... except when she doesn't. The lines often overlap.*

HARRIS. I only have a minute.

ALICE. You're in a hurry?

HARRIS. *(Whipping out his device.)* Yeah.

ALICE. *(Whipping out her folder.)* Me, too.

HARRIS. Great. *(Types or taps, and then realizes that Alice hasn't spoken. His eyes never leave his keyboard. He is a fast typist.)* So whatcha got?

ALICE. *(Reads off her list, looking around the apartment to confirm each detail.)* Renovated pre-war. Open floor plan. Classic SoHo loft. Cast-iron columns, exposed brick walls, soaring thirteen-foot-plus ceilings. Historic architectural details with a modern ... edge —

HARRIS. *(Interrupting Alice, ready to type.)* Co-op? Condo?

ALICE. Cond-op. That's a —

HARRIS. *(Interrupting.)* I know what a —

ALICE. — retail spaces —

HARRIS. — con-dop is.

ALICE. Okay.

HARRIS. *(Interrupting Alice, fingers ready for input.)* Time on market?

ALICE. It's a brand new listing.

HARRIS. *(Typing.)* Price?

ALICE. Two point eight nine five. *(Harris makes an entry.)*

HARRIS. *(Typing.)* Maintenance?

ALICE. Twelve twenty-eight.

HARRIS. *(Entering data.)* Monthly taxes?

ALICE. Eleven thirty-three.

HARRIS. *(Enters that and looks at the total, which his device has calculated.)* Twenty-three sixty-one.

ALICE. *(Almost simultaneously.)* Twenty-three sixty-one.

HARRIS. Financials?

ALICE. No mortgage on the building. High reserve.

HARRIS. Tax abatements?

ALICE. Ended. Nothing coming due.

HARRIS. No outstanding balloon payments?

ALICE. None.

HARRIS. *(Typing.)* The seller?

ALICE. *(A joke.)* Selling. *(Harris doesn't get it.)* Older couple. Retiring to Florida. *(Is quiet while Harris finishes putting in a bit of data.)*

HARRIS. *(Fingers poised to type.)* Square footage?

ALICE. The, uh, square footage. It's on the spec sheet. *(Holds out a brochure, but Harris is engrossed in his device.)* Nineteen hundred. *(Looks at the brochure as Harris types.)* Nineteen and a quarter. *(Harris corrects his entry.)* Nineteen twenty-six, to be exact. *(Harris re-corrects his corrected entry.)* Big.

HARRIS. *(Fingers poised.)* Outside or inside?

ALICE. Excuse me?

HARRIS. *(Finally looking at Alice.)* Was it measured to the inside or to the outside walls?

ALICE. Oh — *(Checks her stats.)*

HARRIS. — Does that include a portion of the common hall-space?

ALICE. It just says nineteen hundred. Nineteen twenty-six.

HARRIS. *(Taps his device to save the entry. Maybe walks across the room, measuring with each step.)* Okay. *(Ready to type again.)* Bedrooms?

ALICE. *(Aha! Maybe now Harris's ready to see the place ... )* Over this way. ( ... Nope. Harris doesn't move, and he keeps his fingers ready to enter data.)

HARRIS. How many bedrooms?

ALICE. Two.

HARRIS. *(Enters a number.)* Baths?

ALICE. Two. *(Harris enters a number.)* And a half.

HARRIS. *(Adds a click.)* Closets?

ALICE. Coat closet in the hallway.

HARRIS. *(His device freezes up. He taps, taps, taps. Typing again.)* How many?

ALICE. *(Making it up as she watches him.)* Six. *(Oblivious to her observation, Harris types. Still making it up.)* Seven, if you count the, um, pantry. *(Sneaks a look to the kitchen to confirm.)* In the kitchen.
HARRIS. *(Without even looking at it.)* New kitchen?
ALICE. Completely renovated.
HARRIS. *(Typing.)* Okay.
ALICE. *(Still watching him.)* Oh, look! *(Inventing.)* "Stanton Style."
HARRIS. *(Doesn't look, but types.)* "Stanton." "Style."
ALICE. *(Looking at notes.)* "Custom cabinets" with … *(Keeps going.)* Parisian knobs. *(No reaction from Harris, who, without looking at the walls or ceiling, has begun to pace out the room dimensions. He is very skilled at this; his stride is exactly one yard long. Impressed, she goes back to her notes.)* "Appliance garage." *(Getting no reply from Harris, she begins to embellish again, as he continues his measurements.)* With a built-in bread maker … "Italian Carrara marble tops" of stone salvaged from Michelangelo's personal rock quarry … "Convection oven" with robotic sous-chef. *(Gives up amusing herself.)*
HARRIS. I don't cook.
ALICE. Lots of take-out places in the neighborhood. *(A beat. Harris is looking at his device but not typing.)* Close to the Village. Not far from the High Line. Close to Tribeca! There's a great dog park nearby.
HARRIS. I don't have a dog.
ALICE. I'm a cat person, too.
HARRIS. Fish.
ALICE. Excuse me?
HARRIS. Fish. I have fish.
ALICE. Oh, nice. Freshwater, saltwater?
HARRIS. Artificial.
ALICE. Really?
HARRIS. They don't die on you.
ALICE. So, no pets.
HARRIS. No. *(Something has shifted.)*
ALICE. You work downtown?
HARRIS. Sometimes.
ALICE. Sometimes? You're a …
HARRIS. Consultant.
ALICE. Consultant?
HARRIS. Management consultant. Here's a card. *(Hands her his card.)*
ALICE. Do you work at home?

HARRIS. When I can. Sometimes Midtown, consulting at different companies. Mostly downtown.

ALICE. Perfect location then. Close to downtown, easy to Midtown. Close to everything!

HARRIS. *(Has finished entering his data and is gathering his things.)* All right then, that's it. Thank you very much. *(Starts to leave.)*

ALICE. You didn't see the apartment.

HARRIS. I've got all the information.

ALICE. You didn't look.

HARRIS. I'm in a hurry.

ALICE. But it's beautiful. *(Noticing the floors for the first time and oblivious to Harris.)* Hardwood floors.

HARRIS. *(Pulls his device out and types.)* "Hardwood floors."

ALICE. *(Staring at the floors.)* Oak.

HARRIS. *(Typing.)* "Oak."

ALICE. *(Addressing his typing.)* No.

HARRIS. *(Typing.)* "No." *(Catches himself.)* Okay. *(Starts to leave again.)* Thanks.

ALICE. *(Looking up.)* Vintage tin cornices. Look. Look!

HARRIS. I really have to leave.

ALICE. Not before you've seen the vintage tin cornices.

HARRIS. *(Looking up.)* Wow.

ALICE. Yes! Look at the detail in this place. It's a really nice kitchen.

HARRIS. Maybe I should learn to cook.

ALICE. There's a wine fridge. Bosch double dishwasher. Side by side. Two dishwashers. *(Harris looks at her.)* For parties. You don't have to wash the dishes as often. *(Harris looks at the dishwashers.)* Or just for everyday. Wash in one, store in the other.

HARRIS. *(Looking at Alice.)* You're different ... from the other realtors.

ALICE. *(Disconcerted, she looks back at her paperwork.)* Um ...

HARRIS. The bedroom?

ALICE. *(Pointing.)* That way.

HARRIS. *(Pokes his head in.)* The bedroom's dark.

ALICE. But that's good. *(Harris looks at her.)* Easier to sleep. There've been studies. It's better to sleep in a dark room.

HARRIS. I need sleep.

ALICE. And a darker bedroom is sexier. *(Oops! A beat. She backtracks.)* And a nice bathroom! *(Checks her notes.)* Albert-Victoria tub. What *is* that, anyway?

HARRIS. A free-standing tub.

ALICE. Oh.

HARRIS. Big enough for two. *(They stare at each other. Alice blushes.)*

ALICE. The master closet's small, but you could … make a walk-in closet from part of the bathroom. *(Makes a mark on the printed floorplan.)* Look at this. Yes, you could. Not a big renovation at all.

HARRIS. *(Comes over to look at the floorplan, which brings them close together.)* You're right. That's a good idea. *(A pause.)*

ALICE. The view. There's a view.

HARRIS. *(Gets out his device. Typing.)* View.

ALICE. No, look.

HARRIS. I've got it.

ALICE. No. LOOK at it. The light. It's … golden.

HARRIS. *(Looks toward the windows for the first time.)* Oh.

ALICE. Magical. *(Looking out.)* Oh, my gosh. What a beautiful view of downtown. *(After a beat.)* This is a great loft.

HARRIS. Yeah.

ALICE. It must be so pretty at night with all the lights, twinkling lights from all the office buildings.

HARRIS. Yeah. *(Looks at the kitchen.)* You know, I don't really need two dishwashers. *(A beat. Alice is still. He turns to go.)*

ALICE. I can show you a triplex in Battery Park City.

HARRIS. *(After a pause.)* I like this one.

ALICE. You do? You do? Well, then.

HARRIS. Best I've seen … *(Takes out his device. Alice is afraid to speak, not certain if she has a deal or not. A pause.)*

ALICE. It's a good investment.

HARRIS. I'm looking for a home, not an investment.

ALICE. I have mortgage charts if you want to run some numbers. Not official, of course, can't do that actually, I'm not a mortgage broker … although I can recommend one to you … not that you have to work with her, you can shop around on your own.

HARRIS. I can pay cash.

ALICE. Really. Cash? Really? Well, the board would love that, wouldn't they! *(Correcting herself.)* Not that it's a really difficult board, not like Park Avenue or anything. They mostly just want to protect their value. It's a great building … artists who've been here for years and business people like yourself … a good mix. Good building.

HARRIS. Yeah.

ALICE. Great loft.

HARRIS. You're right.

ALICE. *(There's nothing else to say.)* Great apartment.

HARRIS. It's perfect.

ALICE. It IS perfect, isn't it.

HARRIS. Best one I've seen. It's great. I love it. *(He and Alice stare at each other. A pause.)*

ALICE. So, where do we stand? *(No answer.)* What's the next move?

HARRIS. I'll call you.

ALICE. When?

HARRIS. I'll call you. *(Starts to gather his things. Alice is nervous and starts talking too much.)*

ALICE. This won't be on the market long. You can make an offer, no down payment required for an offer, but making an offer shows your interest and gets you in the running, and if another offer comes in, well, you saw it first and have the option of raising your bid.

HARRIS. Nope.

ALICE. Okay, I understand you not wanting to get into a bidding war.

HARRIS. Yeah.

ALICE. *(Talking too quickly. She knows it, but she can't stop.)* You know, some people bid really low, and then LATER if you want to be taken seriously and make a real bid you've already damaged the relationship with the seller. *(A pause, as Harris stares at her.)* So are you serious or not? *(A beat.)* How many apartments have you looked at?

HARRIS. *(Casually.)* Couple hundred.

ALICE. A couple hundred?

HARRIS. *(Checking his device.)* Three hundred ninety-six. *(A long pause.)* I'll call you. *(Starts to leave.)*

ALICE. You're not going to take this apartment, are you?

HARRIS. No, I don't think so.

ALICE. Why not?

HARRIS. Just not ... not ... ready ... Maybe there's something else out there ... better ... Just not ready to ... to ... *(Trails off.)*

ALICE. *(After a beat.)* You've taken up most of my day — you were late, you know — and you knew all along you weren't going to buy.

HARRIS. I thought maybe this would be the one.

ALICE. How long have you been looking?

HARRIS. A while. *(A beat.)* Four years.

ALICE. You've seen nearly four hundred apartments in four years and you can't ... decide? Four hundred? You should be a broker!

HARRIS. *(Honestly.)* I've thought about it. Not enough money.

ALICE. You know why? Because we waste our time on people like you! Always shopping, never buying.

HARRIS. But now I've found you.

ALICE. What?

HARRIS. How about we look at something else in SoHo?

ALICE. You're kidding.

HARRIS. There's got to be something even better. You're, you're, you're a really good realtor. Show me some more apartments.

ALICE. No.

HARRIS. That triplex in Battery Park City?

ALICE. Apartment number three hundred ninety-seven? *(Has an epiphany.)* I'm out of here. I'm not going to waste my time on a man who can't commit. I'm too old for that. Got better things to do with my life than spend a whole day with a … with a … Peter Pan kind of guy who can't commit. Can't even commit to real fish. Grow up. *(A pause.)* I'm leaving you. I'm leaving you. Just shut the door behind you, will you? It locks automatically. It's not a great lock, needs to be changed, but I wasn't going to tell you that. Or about all the noise on weekends. And guess what? Do you know about artists' lofts in SoHo? Do you, in all your four hundred apartments, mister? Do you know that there are laws about artists that the city has never invoked? Yes, sir. Laws. On the books. That you have to be an artist to live here. So all these yuppy types like yourself could actually be thrown out of their four-million-dollar lofts. Really. It's true, Mister I'll-Pay-Cash. I just bet you pay cash. You don't have to commit to a mortgage! Mister Businessman. Mister Consultant. Mister Can't-Even-Commit-to-a-Real-Job. *(She is spent. There is a long pause.)*

HARRIS. *(Trying to explain to her.)* My dad was in the military. *(Alice just stares at him.)* My parents moved around a lot. The Army always told us when and where to move.

ALICE. Oh.

HARRIS. The apartment I live in now … the building's been sold. I really have to move. And I really want to move. I have the money. I'd like to be in a new place. But I just can't seem to … I look and look and look … I take notes … I always mean to call the day after, the day after I have the appointment, the very next morning, but I … I … I pick up the card, the realtor's card, and I look at it and I take out my phone, and suddenly I can't even remember what the apartment looked like, or why I thought it would be the one …

I look at my notes ... I look at the card ... and I try to call ... but ... I ... just somehow ... can't ... *(Perhaps he breaks down on Alice's shoulder. Perhaps Alice holds him. Or maybe that's just in their heads. A pause.)*

ALICE. I'm sorry.

HARRIS. Will you help me?

ALICE. What?

HARRIS. Help me.

ALICE. Help you?

HARRIS. Show me some more. Please. Show me another apartment. Co-op, condo. Any price. Anywhere. Please. *(A very long pause, as Alice makes up her mind.)*

ALICE. No. No more. This is it. This is the one.

HARRIS. This one?

ALICE. Yes. This one. We'll close on the twenty-ninth of next month. You'll be moving in three days later.

HARRIS. I will?

ALICE. I'll arrange everything. If there's something you don't like, we'll change it. We'll make it whatever you want it to be.

HARRIS. The city laws? I'm not an artist. I could lose the apartment.

ALICE. That would be tied up in court for years. Probably never happen. You are going to buy this apartment. I'm going to leave now. Here's my card. *(Hands Harris a business card.)* Cell phone, office phone, landline, fax, email, website, LinkedIn, Google Plus, Facebook page, Twitter, and an additional mobile number in case the first one doesn't work. I'm going to leave you alone now, in your new home, and then you are going to call me. You are going to call me — No. No. No. I know. *(Takes her card back.)* I'm going to call YOU. *(Pulls out a previously unseen handheld device, similar to Harris's although maybe not quite as up-to-the-minute, and starts making notes as she walks around the apartment. Harris doesn't take his eyes off her or her device.)* Call Harris. *(To Harris.)* Tomorrow morning. First thing. I'm going to call you, and you are going to bid ten percent above the asking price. Cash. I'll submit your bid tonight. *(Making a note.)* Call banker. *(To Harris.)* And we are going to get this apartment for you. *(Making a note.)* Arrange closing. *(To Harris.)* And I'll hold your hand. I'll get the movers. *(Making a note.)* Call movers. *(To Harris.)* I'll arrange for the movers to pack. *(Making a note.)* Cleaning service. *(To Harris.)* I'll do the unpacking for you. I'll get you a hotel room for a night.

*(Making a note.)* Room at Soho Grand ... *(To Harris.)* ... Or you could go away for a weekend. *(Making a note.)* Check hotels in the Hamptons, no, Sag Harbor. *(To Harris.)* So you don't have to see the boxes. You won't have to do a thing. One day you will be in your little old rental, and a couple of days later you will be in your own home. *(Making a note, getting more and more excited.)* Decorator. *(To Harris.)* I'll have a closet built for you right after the closing. *(Making a note.)* Contractor. *(To Harris.)* A walk-in closet. *(Making a note.)* Call California Closets. *(To Harris.)* I'll arrange the moving. *(Making a note.)* Con Edison. Verizon. I'll pack and unpack your artificial fish. *(To Harris.)* Or a cat. I'll find you a cat.
HARRIS. A puppy. I never had a puppy.
ALICE. *(Continues making notes.)* ASPCA. Dogwalker. Dog trainer. Doggy daycare. *(To Harris.)* You look tired. You might want to take a nap. I'll take care of everything. *(Harris sits on the floor. He takes out his handheld device and places it next to him. Then he lies down on the floor and goes instantly to sleep. She keeps adding to her list.)* Change of address forms. Weekly maid service. List of local restaurants in delivery area. Astor Place Wines: stock wine fridge. New towels and sheets ... Pillows ... *(Looks at Harris sleeping on the floor.)* Lots and lots of fluffy pillows. *(Looks around and smiles.)* Candles. Scented candles. *(Standing very still in the center of the room, she closes her eyes and breathes in the scent of her imagined candles, as Harris continues to sleep, curled up or lying flat on the floor. Eyes closed, they continue to breathe as the lights fade, their chests rising and falling in sync. They are home.)*

**End of Play**

# PROPERTY LIST

iPad
Folder
Brochure
Business cards
Floorplan
Pen
Handheld devices

# FREEFALLING

## BY AURIN SQUIRE

# CHARACTERS

ANTHONY, 35, male.

MICHAEL, 35, male.

STEWARDESS, 35, female.

This fictional play was inspired by
the teachings of Geshe Michael Roach.

FREEFALLING was first produced at Barrington Stage Company
(Julianne Boyd, Artistic Director; Triston Wilson, Managing Director)
in Pittsfield, Massachusetts, as part of the 10x10 Upstreet Arts
Festival in February 2013. It was directed by Julianne Boyd. The cast
was as follows

ANTHONY ........................................................ Dustin Charles
MICHAEL ...................................................... Scott Drummond
STEWARDESS ........................................ Elizabeth Aspenlieder

FREEFALLING went on to win the Fiat Lux Award from the New
York Catholic Church in 2013 and first prize in the Toronto
InspiraTo International Theatre Festival in 2014.

*The plane is going down. Every minute.*
                                    —Geshe Michael Roach

# FREEFALLING

*Anthony, Michael, and Stewardess address the audience in a testimonial.*

ANTHONY. The plane was going down. We had been circling for over an hour, and the pilot said that there was traffic at the gate. Beneath us, beaches glistened in the sun. The stewardesses were obviously disturbed. Sticking their heads in the cockpit:

STEWARDESS. *(In cockpit.)* Is everything all right?

MICHAEL. After ninety minutes of circling, we began to rise. At a ninety degree angle, straight up, really high. And then dive back down in a straight line. This happened three or four times, and people started screaming.

ANTHONY. There is that moment when you realize this could be it. We waited for the pilot to speak to us. But it was the stewardess.

STEWARDESS. Passengers, our landing gear is malfunctioning and we don't quite know if our wheels are down or not. Our pilot has been trying to shake the wheels loose by diving, but the gear light still reads as "up."

MICHAEL. Wonderful. All that technology and we've resorted to "shaking" the wheels like a five-year-old with a toy.

STEWARDESS. So we are left with no choice but to attempt an emergency landing. Hopefully with wheels.

ANTHONY. They know about these things. They know what they're doing.

MICHAEL. Right, they have experience in this.

STEWARDESS. Passengers, we have no experience in doing this. But we're going to do this together. We want to prepare you for an emergency landing.

ANTHONY. This is happening. I'm actually listening to the instructions. Tuck in shoulders. Head between knees.

STEWARDESS. Please remove all jewelry, watches, and belts.

Anything else metallic that can burn your skin. Please also remove your shoes. In case they melt.

MICHAEL. I removed my shoes. These shoes. I bought these at a Foot Locker in Gurnee Mills Malls outside of Chicago.

STEWARDESS. This watch was given to me as a birthday gift by my grandmother. She got it from the Home Shopping Network.

ANTHONY. Passengers start ripping out pieces of paper.

MICHAEL. Love letters and goodbyes. Stuffing them in our underwear, rolling them up into our sleeves. Futility. 'Cause if we burn ...

ANTHONY. I'm hopeful. This is all practice. I'll have a story to tell my children. Speaking of which, I should have some of those. Someone to grieve for me. How selfish. How selfish am I.

MICHAEL. Two kids at home. A gruesome thought occurs to me: now they'll grow up rich. Because of this. This will probably fuck them up. They're too young. The unexpected grief will stun them. They'll be rich, fucked-up adults with addictions and therapy sessions and grief counseling.

STEWARDESS. Passengers, please remember to ...

MICHAEL and ANTHONY. She broke down crying.

STEWARDESS. Suddenly, arms were around me.

MICHAEL. I can't stand to see a woman cry.

ANTHONY. Some strange-looking man from the front row began hugging her. Someone else started crying too. And then another pair of arms was reaching across the aisles.

MICHAEL. Crying, snot, sweat; there were a lot of fluids. I'm pretty sure I smelled piss in the seat next to me. Sweating.

ANTHONY. What's that ammonia smell?

STEWARDESS. I couldn't breathe. So many people were hugging me.

ANTHONY. I've never experienced anything like that. It was like the sun opened up. Each individual just exploded with this warmth ...

MICHAEL. Fluids. It was like a Discovery Channel special just on human fluids. You realize how much of us is so fluid. I guess you only realize that when you're going down.

ANTHONY. I know I wasn't the only who thought this but ... what if we could be like *that* more.

MICHAEL. I had sex the night before. No, not with my wife. I can say that now. I had been having sex regularly with people who were not my wife. She didn't know. I was doing it more for the rush. And none of those experiences compared to this euphoria of dying with other people. Just hugging and touching people, and I felt like a ball of light that was just expanding. Expanding and —

ANTHONY.   — The plane jerked to the right, then zagged to the left. Then the descent began.

MICHAEL.  He was going to try to float it in. Cut off the engines. They've done this before. This seems very shrewd.

STEWARDESS.  It's a gamble. I was in a plane that did this once before. The wind could drag you off course. Or at the last second a downdraft could clip the wings and slam the plane into the runway. You're depending upon angels.

ANTHONY.  The engines cut and it was so silent.

MICHAEL.  Freefalling. Just a hundred tons of steel gliding like a feather. Down and down we went.

STEWARDESS.  He looked at me.

MICHAEL.  I looked at her.

STEWARDESS.  And I remembered that man. The only other time I've been in this situation, and there was this sharply dressed man. Debonair and astute. And he just looks at me and says …

MICHAEL.  God.

STEWARDESS.  God.

MICHAEL.  I wanted that to be the last word on my lips. The last thought in my mind. Not the life insurance premiums or the news coverage or the funeral. I wanted the last word in my soon-to-be-offline brain to be "God." What more is there to say? What more is there to think?

ANTHONY.  I've gone to church every day for the past ten years. I pray every day.

MICHAEL.  I haven't been inside a house of worship since my mom died. And don't believe in it, really. But there it was. Right on my lips at the end.

ANTHONY.  I couldn't think of anything. My throat was dry and choking. No words arose. After all those years of prayer and study, I couldn't even muster a "please" or "God bless." Just this fear. And so I looked at her —

MICHAEL.  I looked at her and said …

STEWARDESS.  I thought of him as this man looked at me.

MICHAEL.  I'm staring down at Chicago. The Sears Tower. Black, tall cylinder against a canvas of gray snow.

ANTHONY.  The waves rushing against the shores. If I get a second chance —

MICHAEL.  — If I get a second chance —

ANTHONY. I would change everything. Marry my first girlfriend.

MICHAEL.  — No regrets. I wouldn't change a thing.

STEWARDESS.  So the last thirty seconds before you hit ground, everything rushes up at you. You actually see people's faces. On one side of the runway was a line of ambulances. And on the other side were —

ANTHONY.  These giant trucks. Hearses. Industrial corpse trucks with these tarps and bags. To pick up the body parts.

MICHAEL.  On one side of the runway there was help, medicine, technology, nurses, these flashing beacons. And on the other side there was just bags to pick up the mess.

ANTHONY.  White stuff on the runway.

MICHAEL.  It's not snow. It's foam.

ANTHONY.  They soak the runway with this foam bubble detergent to soften the landing.

MICHAEL.  I can see the frost on the Chicago light poles.

ANTHONY.  I can see the beads on the palm trees. Welcome to Miami.

MICHAEL.  Our plane caught the ground. And then bounced. We had wheels.

ANTHONY.  At the last moment we turned. And landed on the right wing. The cabin flipped. Light bursts overhead.

MICHAEL.  We skidded through the foam, bubbles disintegrating on my window. We were safe.

ANTHONY.  It was like a can opener peeled back the ceiling. Seats were flying at all angles. And then the last remaining gallons of fuel exploded. Fireball skidding across the runway. Why was I still conscious?

MICHAEL.  The emergency chutes were dropped. And everyone was suddenly laughing, smiling, giving each other backslaps. As if we had done something. We hadn't done anything but sit in our seats.

ANTHONY.  My seat flipped on my side and dragged me on my arm at probably a hundred miles per hour through smoldering luggage, seats with dead passengers, and paper.

STEWARDESS.  It was raining paper and ash. And still I was conscious. Through all the terror.

MICHAEL.  Standing on the runway waiting. The bus was late, and all the laughter and smiles turned to shivers. When the bus arrived, people wanted to get out of the cold. Passengers were shoving each other.

ANTHONY. I tumbled to a stop. My whole right side was shredded. The flesh from my arm had disintegrated and there was just a long white stick attached to my shoulder. And I feel everything melt. But it's a cold melting. Flesh falling like ice cream down the insides of your pants. How can I still be conscious? I'm so cold.

MICHAEL. Once we get inside and start to heat up, it's like nothing happened. We're back on our phones. Business as usual.

STEWARDESS. I had just enough strength to unbuckle my seatbelt. And I fell out of my seat. There he was.

ANTHONY. There she was.

STEWARDESS. I was freezing. The shock of a body losing temperature control. My thoughts jumbled: freezing blood, can't open left eye, something is pouring out of neck.

ANTHONY. She was shaking just as hard as me. I wanted for someone to …

STEWARDESS. I reached out and I grabbed his shoulder.

ANTHONY. It felt so warm. I needed that before I left. I needed some warmth. A touch, some feeling.

STEWARDESS. It was probably my imagination but I thought I saw him smile. He was trying to speak but his mouth was filled with red fluid.

ANTHONY. "Thank you." I kept telling her that. She nodded. Then she closed her eyes. I closed mine. And we died. Together.

STEWARDESS. I was being lifted up to a platform. The screaming was so far away. My body was so far away. I was in pieces. I don't know what part of me they picked up first. And then there was this enormous explosion and I was far above the ambulances and fire. I kept getting farther and farther away until there was only light.

ANTHONY. I felt myself careening. Up. A physiological quirk of a brain going offline? A trick of the mind? And then I see.

STEWARDESS. And then I see.

MICHAEL. Years later I'm sitting in my hotel room watching TV. The money was on the table. She grabbed the cash, got dressed, and split. I turned to CNN and they're doing BREAKING NEWS coverage of a plane crash in Florida. I see her picture flash across the screen. The stewardess. The one from years ago, who I looked in the eyes. On the screen, her ID and picture flashed: Meredith Pena.

STEWARDESS. I see … I see …

MICHAEL. And all of sudden my hand starts shaking and I'm on the floor gasping for air, choking. Either I'm having an asthma atttack or a nervous breakdown … I forgot something. From a long time ago on that Chicago flight, I forgot something. And now I'm gasping on the floor. What did I forget? Something important.

ANTHONY.  I never had a family.

STEWARDESS.  I never forgave my mother.

MICHAEL.  What did I forget?

ANTHONY.  I never learned to play the violin.

STEWARDESS.  I never took a vacation to Hawaii.

MICHAEL.  The plane is going down. All the time. Every minute, every day. I've tried to block out that day or Meredith.

STEWARDESS.  Our chests cracked open. We were light.

ANTHONY.  We flew together. Up into the clouds and finally remembered. Remembered who we were, who we are, and who we will always be.

MICHAEL.  I was on my knees, rocking back and forth. I raised my hands to the ceiling. And for the first time in years … I wept. Thank you. Thank you, I remember now.

**End of Play**

# POISON

## BY JOHN PATRICK SHANLEY

## CHARACTERS

GYPSY, a fortune-teller.

KELLY, a professional woman in her 30s.

KENNY, Kelly's ex; a decent guy in his 30s.

## SETTING

The fortune-teller's parlor, and Kelly's apartment.

# POISON

*Kelly sits with a fortune-teller in low light. They hold hands.*

*The fortune-teller gasps as she takes on Kelly's psyche.*

GYPSY.  What do you want to know?

KELLY.  Can I get him back?

GYPSY.  No.

KELLY.  I don't believe you.

GYPSY.  Fine.

KELLY.  He loved me!

GYPSY.  Yes he did. But then you showed him something bad, and he can never forget that.

KELLY.  I had too much to drink. It was one night.

GYPSY.  The thing he saw, it's always there.

KELLY.  What is it?

GYPSY.  You hate yourself.

KELLY.  No. Yes. But I wouldn't if he loved me. *(The fortune-teller says nothing.)* I've got to get him back.

GYPSY.  You should go on a long trip, alone, maybe to India. You should face yourself.

KELLY.  I'm not going to do that.

GYPSY.  Okay.

KELLY.  I know myself.

GYPSY.  Okay.

KELLY.  I can't be alone. I go crazy when I'm alone. I tear myself to pieces.

GYPSY.  You're going to get ill if you keep on this path. Something will go wrong with your gallbladder.

KELLY.  Look, don't tell me any more about the future. It makes me sick. Tell me how to get what I want.

GYPSY.  What do you want?

KELLY. I want him back. I want him to love me again, like he did before. *(A pause.)*
GYPSY. There may be a way.
KELLY. What?
GYPSY. I could give you something to give to him.
KELLY. You mean like a love potion?
GYPSY. No. It's a poison.
KELLY. What?
GYPSY. You cannot make true love happen. But there are things you can do.
KELLY. I don't want to kill him. I want to love him.
GYPSY. This poison kills a man's soul. *(A pause.)*
KELLY. What good would that do me?
GYPSY. The bad thing he saw in you, if his soul is dead, he won't see it anymore.
KELLY. Can't you just make him love me?
GYPSY. You don't want love. You've had that. It doesn't satisfy you. You want power. You want this man to be bound to you.
KELLY. I don't know. What would that look like?
GYPSY. He would do anything to please you. He would be afraid of you.
KELLY. And if I don't give this stuff to him?
GYPSY. He will marry his yoga instructor.
KELLY. Wait a minute. He doesn't have a yoga instructor. He doesn't go to yoga.
GYPSY. He will. And he will marry the instructor.
KELLY. That must not happen.
GYPSY. He would be happier.
KELLY. Who cares?! What about me? Does my happiness count for nothing?!
GYPSY. You don't have any happiness.
KELLY. That's right. Do you have this stuff? *(The fortune-teller takes out a small can.)*
GYPSY. Give him this.
KELLY. *"Go"?* This is an energy drink.
GYPSY. A thousand dollars.
KELLY. A thousand dollars for a ginseng-flavored soda?
GYPSY. And another thousand when it works.
KELLY. Does he have to drink the whole thing?
GYPSY. No. Three sips. Then knock it out of his hand.

KELLY. Or what?

GYPSY. On the third sip, his soul will die. But on the fourth, his heart will stop.

KELLY. Death?

GYPSY. Three sips and knock it out of his hand.

KELLY. Okay. How will I know it worked?

GYPSY. You'll know.

KELLY. How?

GYPSY. He'll be like you. He'll hate himself. *(The lights crossfade on Kelly's apartment. The door buzzer rings. Kelly walks into the scene. She bustles, putting on a robe. It's Kenny. Kenny knocks impatiently. We hear him.)*

KENNY. *(Offstage.)* Kelly, are you all right? Open the door. Kelly? *(Kelly opens the door.)*

KELLY. Hi, Kenny, I'm sorry I'm such a mess. I'm sorry I had to call you.

KENNY. Are you okay?

KELLY. Thanks for coming.

KENNY. You sounded terrible.

KELLY. I'm pretty bad.

KENNY. Well. You need to talk to somebody, Kelly.

KELLY. I know. That's why I called you.

KENNY. I mean a professional.

KELLY. I know. I will. It's just late, and you can't get those people after-hours. You just get a recording that says go to an emergency room. I'll get in there first thing Monday.

KENNY. Good.

KELLY. Can I get you something?

KENNY. No.

KELLY. Hi.

KENNY. Hi.

KELLY. Just sit with me a bit, okay?

KENNY. Sure. *(They sit at a dining table.)* This place seems so unlived in.

KELLY. I never really moved in. I thought I'd just be here a few months. And now look. It's three years.

KENNY. You oughta get a dog or something.

KELLY. Then I couldn't travel.

KENNY. Travel? You? You never go anywhere.

KELLY. I'm thinking about going to India.

KENNY.  Really? Wow.

KELLY.  Yeah.

KENNY.  Good for you.

KELLY.  It's time I faced myself. I can't go on like I have, that's for sure.

KENNY.  I'm so sorry, Kelly.

KELLY.  You're such a nice guy, Kenny, such a good man.

KENNY.  I'm all right. You're a terrific person. You shouldn't get so down on yourself.

KELLY.  I know.

KENNY.  The fact that it didn't work out between us is sad, but these feelings pass.

KELLY.  I'm just not that good at being alone.

KENNY.  But you've mostly been alone.

KELLY.  Right. And I'm not that good at it.

KENNY.  Maybe you should try yoga.

KELLY.  What? What do you know about yoga?

KENNY.  I just started. I really like it.

KELLY.  Really? Let me get you something to drink.

KENNY.  Nothing alcoholic.

KELLY.  No. It's just an energy drink.

KENNY.  I'd better not. It might keep me up.

KELLY.  Not that kind. It's just vitamins and water. Refreshing.

KENNY.  Okay. *(Kelly pours the contents of the can into a glass.)*

KELLY.  It's nice stuff.

KENNY.  *(Takes a sip, puts it down.)* It's good.

KELLY.  That's one.

KENNY.  One what?

KELLY.  One good thing about me. At least I'm hospitable. I give you something to drink.

KENNY.  Oh, come on. There's a lot of good things about you.

KELLY.  So who was your yoga instructor?

KENNY.  Some woman. She had great skin.

KELLY.  You noticed her skin?

KENNY.  Yeah. She had that yoga glow.

KELLY.  Oh. Yeah.

KENNY.  You sounded so bad on the phone. You don't seem so bad now.

KELLY.  It was being alone. I'm not good at it.

KENNY.  Yeah, I know that one. But the more you run away, the more you just keep bumping into yourself.

KELLY. How's the job?

KENNY. It's okay. To tell you the truth, I don't care about work that much. Don't get me wrong. I'll always work, but other things are more important to me.

KELLY. Like what?

KENNY. Quality of life.

KELLY. You mean like home life?

KENNY. Yeah. A home. *(Takes another sip.)*

KELLY. That's two.

KENNY. Two what?

KELLY. Too perfect. That your home life's important to you. I mean, you're just that kind of guy. You know, home. Speaks so well of you. Are you religious?

KENNY. Not particularly.

KELLY. Do you believe in the soul? Do you believe you have a soul?

KENNY. Oh, yeah.

KELLY. What's it for?

KENNY. Well. When you die, it's the part that goes on. And while you're alive, it's the part that tells you which way you should go.

KELLY. So it's the part that told you to break up with me?

KENNY. Come on with that. I didn't say that. *(Raises the glass to take a third sip. Kelly seizes his wrist.)*

KELLY. Wait. Before you take that … sip … Kenny, what do you want?

KENNY. *(Tenderly takes her hand.)* Well, what do you think? I want you to be happy, Kelly. I want you to give up the dark stuff and start to enjoy life.

KELLY. Then come back to me.

KENNY. Don't.

KELLY. I'm sorry. It just slipped out. I'm always saying stuff I shouldn't.

KENNY. Was that phone call to me real, or were you just angling?

KELLY. It was real. I'm in trouble.

KENNY. Maybe I'd better go.

KELLY. Not yet. Give me a couple of minutes. Is that too much to ask? Let's make this a smooth landing, okay?

KENNY. Okay. *(A pause.)*

KELLY. Do you think some souls are no good?

KENNY. What do you mean?

KELLY. I mean, when a person is evil, do you think that's because the soul of that person is bad?

KENNY. I don't think I believe in evil.

KELLY. Oh, there's evil. Like when a person will do anything, kill beautiful things, just to get her way.

KENNY. *Her* way?

KELLY. Then maybe her soul is no good.

KENNY. Kelly, promise me you'll make an appointment and talk to somebody.

KELLY. I'm thirsty. Let me have that. *(Takes Kenny's drink and drinks one, two, three sips.)* One.

KENNY. Why do you keep counting anyway? *(Kelly laughs.)* Wait a minute. Is there something in there?

KELLY. Three.

KENNY. Did you spike it with something?

KELLY. It takes three sips. You only had two.

KENNY. What the fuck are you talking about?

KELLY. You can't kill what was never alive. If your soul is dead, you can't kill it.

KENNY. You're crazy.

KELLY. But you can stop your heart. You can end the pain and the drama. With a fourth sip. *(Drains the glass.)*

KENNY. I shouldn't have come here.

KELLY. Oh, you need to be here.

KENNY. What for?

KELLY. Watch and see. And remember this, Kenny. Because this is your fault.

KENNY. What's my fault? What's happening?

KELLY. I'm dying.

KENNY. You are?

KELLY. Look at me.

KENNY. I don't see anything.

KELLY. What do you mean?

KENNY. Nothing's happening. *(Kelly realizes she isn't dying.)*

KELLY. What do you mean nothing's happening?! Motherfucker. That gypsy!

KENNY. What gypsy?

KELLY. Get out.

KENNY. What's the matter with you?

KELLY. I'm alive! I'm still alive!

KENNY.  You need to talk to somebody.

KELLY.  Do I?

KENNY.  Oh, yes!

KELLY.  Maybe I do!

KENNY.  Are you okay?

KELLY.  Perfect.

KENNY.  You're nuts.

KELLY.  I'm fine.

KENNY.  You're not going to do something stupid, are you?

KELLY.  I already have. Now go. Follow your soul. Go to yoga.

KENNY.  You should try it!

KELLY.  Never!

KENNY.  Okay. Good night.

KELLY.  Good night, Kenny. *(She has hustled Kenny out the door. He's gone. She runs into the next scene. She's back in the fortune-teller's parlor. Bangs on the table.)* Come out! Show your face!

GYPSY.  What are you doing here?

KELLY.  You cheated me!

GYPSY.  You need an appointment.

KELLY.  I'm alive.

GYPSY.  You drank the potion? It wasn't for you!

KELLY.  Yes, I drank it! One, two, three, and then all the rest of it. All of it! And I'm alive!

GYPSY.  No, you're a dead woman. You were dead when you showed up here.

KELLY.  You took my money!

GYPSY.  You can't force people to love you!

KELLY.  He's not going to humiliate me!

GYPSY.  Here! Take your money then! I don't want it. Get out!

KELLY.  No. I don't want my money. I want him back! I want my boyfriend back!

GYPSY.  As a slave to you? Like a dog who comes when you call?

KELLY.  Any way I can get him. And you can help me. You have powers. You knew about the yoga teacher.

GYPSY.  You should have gone to India.

KELLY.  What good would that have done?

GYPSY.  You would have eaten a rotten curry and died of food poisoning!

KELLY.  You bitch! India. You were trying to kill me!

GYPSY.  It would have been better.

KELLY.  Help me get him back.

GYPSY.  Don't you understand? You can't have this. You want something that you can't have. I told you that. You wouldn't listen. So I told you what you wanted to hear. But none of this matters because you are a dead woman. That's why you can't be poisoned. Because you are dead already.

KELLY.  We'll see who's dead! *(Pulls out a knife.)*

GYPSY.  A knife?! Are you insane? What are you doing? Put that away!

KELLY.  Did you foresee this? Huh?

GYPSY.  I'll give you money.

KELLY.  I don't want money. I want love!

GYPSY.  You crazy bitch!

KELLY.  Give me love!

GYPSY.  All right. I will help you.

KELLY.  You're scared. You're lying.

GYPSY.  No. There's a way.

KELLY.  Tell me.

GYPSY.  Kill him.

KELLY.  What?

GYPSY.  Take that knife and kill him. Cut his throat.

KELLY.  What are *you* talking about?

GYPSY.  Because that's the only way, the only way you can have him. *(Kelly drops the knife, falls to her knees, starts to cry.)*

KELLY.  Why was I born? *(The fortune-teller stands over her.)*

GYPSY.  You were born for this moment. *(Grabs Kelly by the hair.)* You were born in this moment.

KELLY.  Let me go!

GYPSY.  Hear me now, my little one. Hear me as you could not before. You must be alone.

KELLY.  Why?

GYPSY.  Because everyone must.

KELLY.  But I don't want to.

GYPSY.  No one does.

KELLY.  All right. I will be alone.

GYPSY.  Good girl.

KELLY.  Did you know it would end this way?

GYPSY.  I hoped it would. But life is strange. Now get out. *(Kelly heads for the door.)* But before you go, one thousand dollars!

**End of Play**

# PROPERTY LIST

Small can of energy drink
Glass
Knife


# SOUND EFFECTS

Door buzzer

# SELF-TORTURE AND STRENUOUS EXERCISE

## BY HARRY KONDOLEON

# CHARACTERS

ALVIN

BETHANY

CARL

ADEL

# SETTING

Fall. Late.

The dining room of Alvin and Bethany. There is a round table with a white tablecloth and the remnants of a late-night supper. There are dirty plates, half-filled glasses, unfolded napkins, unlit candles, and a centerpiece of flowers. As much occurs on the floor, a raked stage would be an asset.

# SELF-TORTURE AND STRENUOUS EXERCISE

*Carl, Alvin, and Bethany are seated at the table.*

CARL.  Alvin, I'm in love with another woman.

ALVIN.  Good! Good for you Carl. I'm glad. When Adel died, I can't tell you the psychic exhaustion I suffered worrying who you'd find to take her place. I didn't want to cook. Tell him, Beth. I just stood at my cutting board, surrounded by raw vegetables, and thought, why go on? I wanted a sign from above. I wanted God to say, "Al, go on." Death is so depleting. I know you loved Adel, but did you know I did? I loved her. I don't mean I was sleeping with her — I loved her as a spiritual sister, are you following me? Then I thought how everything goes back to the mixing bowl. How we cannot expect to be given any clues to God's great recipe. Follow? And then I picked up my knife, ready to cut again, and thought, Adel is back in God's kitchen: There is no call for mourning.

CARL.  Alvin, I've told you one hundred times, Adel *attempted* suicide. She was *not* successful. She is still *alive*, and the two of us have *separated*. Do you understand? Adel lives. Adel lives, and I am in love with another woman.

ALVIN.  And I'm glad! I'm happy. I look down at our dirty plates, some bones and fat left over, some pits from fruit, I look down at these plates and I say, "God bless us!" Do you know what I'm getting at, Carl?

BETHANY.  I feel dizzy. I need to lie down. I'm going to lie down. *(She lies down on the floor, mummylike.)*

CARL.  I'm in love with your wife!

ALVIN.  I look at these dirty plates, and I think, "God! Aren't *we* the dirty plates?" Aren't we the plates who have been taken off the shelf, heaped with little portions of prepared nourishment, eaten off of, finally laid on the table, dirty and waiting to be taken back into the kitchen to be cleaned, and what? — used again! And again! The life cycle! Revival! Hope! Divine design!

CARL. Alvin, I'm in love with your wife, Beth. *I love her.*

ALVIN. But of course you love her! It's the most natural thing in the world. What could be more natural? You love her and you love me, and she loves you and she loves me, and I love you both. And before Adel died, we all loved her.

CARL. Adel is alive. I love Beth. I love her and want her. I want to go away with her.

ALVIN. I'm not surprised! With Adel gone — though in your grief you temporarily block her burial — you look to new female companionship. What could be more natural? It goes without saying. You see Bethany as surrogate female companionship, am I right? And look — Beth in her beauty and acceptance has sought to duplicate the position of dead Adel. *Look* what she's doing for you, Carl. Now how can you say we don't love you?

BETHANY. The floor is turning under me. Just me. Your floor is still. My floor is moving.

ALVIN. Bethany, would you like another glass of wine? A mint?

CARL. Alvin, I wish you'd just sit still for one minute and try to get all this information straight. A) I'm in love with Beth and Beth's in love with me; B) Beth and I have been sleeping together for several years — long before I left Adel; and C) Beth and I want to go away together, live and love together. Is it all clear now? You understand?

ALVIN. You love Beth and Beth loves you, you've slept with Beth and Beth's slept with you, you want to go away with Beth and Beth wants to go away with you. I understand.

BETHANY. Make something matter. Somebody make something matter.

CARL. Beth, get up off the floor and we'll go away together. Alvin understands.

BETHANY. I can't.

CARL. Alvin understands. He says he understands.

ALVIN. What's there not to understand?

BETHANY. I can't.

CARL. Beth!

BETHANY. I can't. I can't get up.

CARL. Let me help you.

BETHANY. No!

CARL. Beth! What are you saying? Are you saying you don't want to go away with me? After all this time? After years?

BETHANY. I can't get up. I'm stuck.

CARL. Get up!

ALVIN. Can I get you a pillow? A blanket, Beth? There's an autumn chill that seeps right in through the floor — not having a basement, the dampness of the earth becomes a problem for us.

CARL. *Beth, get up!* Our plans, think of our plans! The down payments on the cottage, your return to poetry, my new novel!

ALVIN. Down payments? Poetry? A new novel?

CARL. Beth! What's wrong with you? Alvin, did you give her something? Did you put something in her wine? Or food?

ALVIN. A new novel, Carl? I'm so glad. I thought perhaps with the tragedy of Adel you'd get blocked. You're turning a new leaf?

CARL. Why is she acting so peculiar — did you add something to the food?

ALVIN. Carl, I put lots of things in the food. I was at the range all day, mixing things in bowls, adding this and that — all intuitively.

CARL. What is going on here?

ALVIN. This afternoon I was out picking the last string beans from the vines. These were late beans — did you think them coarse?

CARL. Beth, what are you doing? Are you turning this into a joke? Adel tried to *kill* herself when she found out about us, and you're turning the whole thing into a joke! Bethany!

ALVIN. I stood there among these late vines — late beans — and thought, my God! the glory of nature! I mean, I was picking beans that later that same day we would be consuming. Chewing and eating the same beans that hours previously hung at the mercy of a changing season. You follow? I think the vines thanked me, taking in their children before the autumn chill. I felt blessed, special. When Beth and I moved into this house, I debated the idea of a city garden. All that extra work, I thought. I hadn't foreseen the spiritual feedback. And now *you* have a new leaf, Carl. Tell us about it.

BETHANY. *(Still recumbent.)* You're a stingy writer, Carl. You have one barely articulated point of view projected on too many thinly-disguised characters.

CARL. Bethany!

BETHANY. *The Motel of the Heart*? With all those characters? They were really one character, they all had one problem, one point of view.

CARL. What are you saying?

ALVIN. Beth's an insightful critic.

BETHANY. The character of Georgette? You meant to base her on me. But it wasn't me, Carl. It was you. When Georgette says she doesn't know how to love, that she flies from one set of arms to the next in the desperate hope of finding the right pair, it is you speaking, Carl, your search for the right pair. I lie here, and I say nothing matters. I shout, somebody make something matter! And in your next book, Carl, you'll call me Renata or Thalia, and I'll be standing in a train station; my lover will appear, and I, dropping my handbag, my overnight bag, my little wax bag of grapes, will fall into my lover's arms and say — moan — bring me back to life, resurrect me in your house of love.

CARL. What is all this about? Is this a joke, a joke on me?

ALVIN. Don't interrupt.

BETHANY. I can't tell you the death I feel when I see myself disguised in your books, Carl. When I see you playing me.

CARL. Don't say this! Don't say this! You're torturing me. I love you. I'd never do anything to hurt you.

BETHANY. And Adel? Where *is* Adel now?

CARL. Adel is home!

ALVIN. Oh, the perversity of grief!

BETHANY. It's you, Carl, you standing in the train station with the bags, with the beaten thesaurus in the overnight bag.

CARL. You're not yourself!

BETHANY. Every writer comes to a point of breakthrough. When he sees the lies from the lies, the Georgettes from the Georgettes.

CARL. I love you!

ALVIN. You're not well, Carl. The emotional strain. The absence of Adel. Your new book. Too much. Don't you think I noticed how you more or less *pecked* at your food, Carl?

CARL. Bethany!

BETHANY. The floor is moving under me. I'm moving.

CARL. You're speaking nonsense deliberately — you're trying to drive me off — you're *testing* me. But I won't be tricked. I'm taking you away, and if you won't get up I'll pick you up.

ALVIN. *(Scraping a plate.)* Carl, you're torturing yourself!

CARL. Beth, I'm going to pick you up and carry you away!

ALVIN. You can't pick her up.

BETHANY. A weak novelist. *(Carl picks Bethany up and carries her like a bride.)*

ALVIN. You're picking her up!

BETHANY. I'm being picked up. I'm in the air now, Alvin. There's nothing I can do. I'm being carried away. You'll know I didn't walk out on you.

CARL. *(Moving toward the door.)* We're going now. *(Bethany and Carl exit.)*

ALVIN. Wait! Wait! I can't believe this. What about the autumn vegetables? What about me? Beth! The pumpkins! Beth, the pumpkins aren't ready yet. Pumpkin pie, pumpkin pancakes, pumpkin seeds — Beth, where are you going? Carl! Beth! Come back! In the spring everything will be in bloom! *(Sits back at his place at the table, considers what has happened.)* Well, that sure took me for a loop. Just whisked her off the floor. Guess who's left with the dishes? Times like this I think of my mother and my father. I reconsider them. I think of my mother, who said, "No matter how well you prepare a meal, no guest will ever fully appreciate it." And I think of my father, who, the day after my mother died, thought with a sudden sense of profound despair as he dropped a frozen pouch into a pot of boiling water, "I loved that woman, I loved her!" *(Enter Adel. Her hair and clothing are disheveled, her makeup smudged. Her wrists are thickly wrapped in white gauze.)*

ADEL. Where is the fucker?!

ALVIN. An apparition! Dear God in heaven.

ADEL. What? Alvin, it's me, Adel. Where's Carl?

ALVIN. Adel! Adel! You're *alive!*

ADEL. Of course I'm alive! I'm here, aren't I?

ALVIN. I'm in shock, Adel.

ADEL. Where's Carl? Carl and Beth?

ALVIN. They went away, Adel. You didn't see them? Carl was holding Beth.

ADEL. Then that was them! I saw somebody with a bundle running down the street.

ALVIN. That was them.

ADEL. Is it too late to catch them?

ALVIN. Adel, you're really alive. I thought you were dead.

ADEL. That's because Carl wants me dead!

ALVIN. Carl said that you were alive.

ADEL. Carl wants to kill me, Alvin!

ALVIN. No.

ADEL. Yes!

ALVIN. Carl?

ADEL. Yes, Alvin. Carl wants everything in his path dead. He wants you dead too, Alvin. He's probably telling Beth right now that you're dead.

ALVIN. But I'm alive, Adel.

ADEL. I know, Alvin, but we're talking about *Carl*. Don't you know who Carl is?

ALVIN. I know Carl.

ADEL. I hate him! Look at me, Alvin. I'm a mess! And who's made me a mess?

ALVIN. Who?

ADEL. *Carl!* Don't you know what he's done to me? How he sucked me dry and then tried to bury the evidence? Do you know what I'm talking about, Alvin?

ALVIN. No, Adel, I really don't.

ADEL. I'm talking about seven years! Seven years with a bloodsucker! You don't think I have scars, Alvin? I have them! I've kept them from people — out of embarrassment and humiliation! I've had to keep my true self down to accommodate Carl.

ALVIN. Accommodate Carl?

ADEL. Who do you think wrote *The Motel of the Heart*? Carl? Carl can't even spell! I wrote *The Motel of the Heart*, and he stole it! Right out of my head!

ALVIN. Adel, this is so baffling.

ADEL. What's baffling? *(Opening her locket, a kind of pillbox on a chain around her neck, she pops some Valium. This action does not interrupt the lines.)* That Carl has used terrorist tactics to publish a novel? You don't know the real Carl, Alvin. You don't know how this sort of man operates! You have any extra Valium in the house? — I'm running low.

ALVIN. Adel, I don't have Valium, and I don't think badly of Carl. All people are good at heart, Adel. Even in times of severe strife you must not forget this. I do understand that you must feel a little cut off from things right now, but we can't blame our spouses for our shortcomings, Adel. I'm positive Carl wants to reconcile himself to you, that he still loves you deep in his heart and will share his royalties with you. Carl is very spur-of-the-moment. He and Beth will be back — they've only gone out for a short walk or something. A vacation is all Carl needs. Being a creative artist ...

ADEL. Carl is *not* a creative artist! He's a destructive journalist! His novels are no more than a "misconstruance" of the affairs he himself perpetrates on the people around him. Because my love *blinded* me, I have been *duped* into transforming his vile logs into the kindling of fiction. Don't you see the evil? *I'm* the creative one, Alvin! I've been tricked — we've all been manipulated for Carl's personal gain! Don't you see how one by one Carl will attempt to wipe out those who *know*. Don't you see, Alvin, that unless we — the Anti-Carls — mass together, we will face extinction! *(Picking up a platter with a cake on it. It has one slice missing.)* Pretend this is us, Alvin, our kind — *(A quick sniff.)* What is this, cheesecake? — watch me. *(She raises her fist and brings it down violently onto the cake. The cake splatters.)* That's what they want to do to us!

ALVIN. I don't think God would ever permit such a thing, Adel.

ADEL. God has nothing to do with this! You think God cares about bestseller lists and ripped-off wives? Alvin, I am telling you, they want to wipe us out!

ALVIN. They? *Who* are you talking about, Adel?

ADEL. Carl! You don't think he works alone, do you? Not at this point in his rise to recognition. He has *people*! Hired people! They follow me, Alvin. They know my every move! They followed me here on the bus!

ALVIN. You didn't take a taxi?

ADEL. I did! They took the bus. *(She is fishing through her pockets and bag. The bag empties itself onto the floor.)* Where'd I put my Valium? They must have known I was coming here! You didn't tell anyone, did you?

ALVIN. Adel, until a few minutes ago I thought you were dead. *(Adel dives under the table to search through her things.)*

ADEL. *(Her head bobbing up for a moment.)* That's my point exactly! You don't know the hell I've been living these past weeks. Pure hell! *(She bobs down under again.)* If I don't find my Valium in one minute, I'm going to die right here. Alvin! Come down and help me! *(Alvin descends.)*

ALVIN. Here it is, Adel! I found your Valium.

ADEL. That's my lipstick. Keep looking. *(Leaping up.)* I found them! Help me collect this junk. Only two left. I need two. I had two in the taxi.

ALVIN. You need something to drink with that?

ADEL. No, I take 'em dry. I've gotten to the point where I can't depend on a ready water supply. *(They are both off the floor now. Adel is stuffing her things back into her bag. She remembers her locket.)* Oh, Jesus! I forgot my locket!

ALVIN. Save those for an emergency, Adel.

ADEL. This is an emergency. *(Noticing the leftovers.)* What'd you serve? Is that lamb?

ALVIN. Oh, Adel, I made —

ADEL. Listen to me, Alvin — I'm talking about my life! I came here to *kill* Carl! How much longer do you think I have, Alvin? How much longer before Carl gets me? Do you know he threatened to pull my stitches out? He did! I had to ward him off with the dogs — Prince and King. The next day he let them go. He said, "I'm going to release the dogs," as if it was Bastille Day or something. My only source of protection let out on the street to be run over ... "Why don't you release yourself, Carl?" I said. "Go stand in front of a truck!"

ALVIN. Adel, you don't mean these things!

ADEL. Don't I? You know what I have in my pocket, Alvin? Guess!

ALVIN. Valium?

ADEL. A letter! A letter to Carl!

ALVIN. You've written Carl a letter?

ADEL. No! It's a letter from a literary society. It came today.

ALVIN. You didn't open it, Adel, did you?

ADEL. Of course I did! What are you thinking of?! I opened it, and I read it, and do you know what it says? *(Brandishing the letter.) The Motel of the Heart* has won some national book award. There's an invitation to a ceremonial banquet!

ALVIN. A ceremonial banquet! How marvelous, Adel! A gift from God. I'm so happy for Carl — and for you, Adel. Surely Carl will take you to the banquet.

ADEL. Alvin, I think you've been sitting in the kitchen too long. You're not seeing anything clearly! Do you still not know that Carl was sleeping with — fucking with — your wife, Beth? Years, he said! Years! Of deception! What do I care about banquets!

ALVIN. God, Adel, I would think —

ADEL. I'm talking about *Satan*, and you keep bringing up God! I'm telling you, Carl is the maker of all things evil on this planet — all betrayal, mockery, and injustice! *(Banging her elbows, since she hesitates to use her fists, on the table for emphasis. Some glasses may fall over.)* Carl must be destroyed! Time is running out! He will take over the world!

ALVIN. Adel, I *insist* that you calm down. You're beginning to distort things.

ADEL. You mean relax? *Relax.* That's what my doctor says. "Relax, Adel," she says, "relax and stop persecuting yourself with self-analysis. Just relax." *(Picking up a fork and demurely sampling some splattered cake.)* Yuck! *(She flings the fork away.)* That's too sweet!

ALVIN. Beth did the cake.

ADEL. *(Spitting it out.)* Tastes like poison.

ALVIN. It is sweet.

ADEL. I don't blame Beth. Though I wrote and typed *The Motel of the Heart* and it was dedicated to her — I don't blame her.

ALVIN. Well, that's good, Adel. The less blame and animosity you have, the better.

ADEL. *(Pushing the cake platter aside.)* Alvin, I've been working on a *new* novel. Did you know?

ALVIN. No.

ADEL. Well, I have. An exposé! An exposé novel on Carl.

ALVIN. Sounds absorbing, Adel.

ADEL. It is. I'm exerting the smallest effort to disguise Carl's identity. Soon the world will see this great minor writer as the forger and bloodsucker he really is!

ALVIN. You have the book with you?

ADEL. It's in my head. All I have to do is *type* it! I carry all my notes here, near my bosom. *(She takes out a small packet of notes.)*

ALVIN. It's so little, Adel.

ADEL. It's in code! And it's going to stay in code until I can find a safe place.

ALVIN. A safe place?

ADEL. Yes, Alvin!

ALVIN. Right before my mother died, she said that. She took my hand and said, "Alvin, I'm going to a safe place."

ADEL. I need that place, Alvin! *(She leans over to take Alvin's hand and accidently knocks over a decanter of wine. It crashes to the floor. She jumps.)* You see! The peril of every moment! Things seeking my destruction! Alvin, I must write my exposé before it's too late —

Let me move in here — now that Beth's gone, you have lots of room. I won't be any trouble. I'll type real quiet. I'll do the dishes. Say yes, Alvin — save my life!

ALVIN. All right, Adel, I listened to you, now have another Valium and listen to me. Carl is good at heart — yes, Adel! Listen to what I have to tell, Adel. Carl may have gone astray, but he is *not* a bad man. He and Beth have probably just gone out for a walk — *(Adel attempts an outburst. Alvin cuts her off.)* — or maybe they just went away for the weekend — there is no sin in a short holiday.

ADEL. Short holiday?! They are fornicating right this minute on some front lawn!

ALVIN. Silence, Adel! Listen to me. Perhaps Carl went temporarily insane with the belief of your death.

ADEL. Alvin, he didn't believe I was dead — you did. He wants me dead, but he knows I'm not.

ALVIN. Adel, listen to me. I'm going to take my car out and bring back Bethany and Carl. Then we'll discuss this all together.

ADEL. How are you going to find them?

ALVIN. They couldn't have gotten very far. Carl was carrying Beth.

ADEL. You're going to bring Carl back? Don't tell him about the letter; let me.

ALVIN. Okay, Adel, but you have to promise to calm down, okay?

ADEL. Relax. I know ... "Relax, Adel." Alvin, before you go, could you get me something?

ALVIN. Adel, I told you we have no tranquilizers in the house.

ADEL. No. Hot water. Could you bring me a bowl of hot water and a washcloth? And soap.

ALVIN. You want to bathe? Why don't you use the bathroom, Adel?

ADEL. Don't ask.

ALVIN. I'll get it for you. *(He exits.)*

ADEL. *(To herself. Between lines, she picks at leftover food with increasing speed and appetite.)* Carl thinks he's rid of me! Perhaps Carl will come back. I don't need Carl! But I still love Carl! I should sacrifice myself to a man who is unfaithful, manipulative, and self-centered? But sometimes he's so gentle and understanding and strong. You want to be choked by him? No, but I like when Carl holds me. *(Alvin enters quickly with a silver tray on which is a bowl of hot water, a washcloth, and a bar of soap. He places it on the table.)*

ALVIN. Here you are, Adel. Try not to make a puddle. I'll be back as soon as I find them. Now, you're not depressed or anything, are you?

ADEL. No.

ALVIN. Good. See you in no time. *(Alvin exits. Adel washes herself. After some moments Bethany enters, crawling on her hands and knees.)*

BETHANY. Carl is a trap. *(Adel, surprised, jumps and drops her bowl of water.)*

ADEL. Beth, is that you?

BETHANY. Adel! Adel, you are here! Forgive! Forgive me, Adel!

ADEL. You're not with Carl?

BETHANY. Carl is a trap! I know that now. He stopped at a phone booth to call his agent and found out about some book award. He started leaping and clapping in the booth and then went on to make over a dozen calls, while he left me lying on the sidewalk. As I was lying there among the dead leaves, I realized what a conceited shithead Carl really is and, more important, how I have transgressed against you, Adel.

ADEL. Me?

BETHANY. When I started to crawl home — I couldn't stand — Carl was still on the phone. He probably doesn't even know that I've left him. Adel, your shoes are all wet.

ADEL. I've been bathing.

BETHANY. Let me dry them! *(She uses her hair to dry Adel's shoes.)*

ADEL. Your hair! You don't have to do that, Beth.

BETHANY. I want to! I want forgiveness! Will you give it to me, Adel? Will you?

ADEL. Does Carl know I'm here?

BETHANY. *(Wringing her hair.)* Carl is a trap!

ADEL. *(Avoiding Bethany's grip.)* My whole life has become a trap, Beth! Every day I wake up, and there's a trap. I don't mean just *traps* — I mean *real* traps. I mean, I can't get from my bed to the kitchen without things falling in my path — falling on my head! I try to be careful, I try to take things slowly, watch where I'm going, but — POW! I get it. Glasses fall from the shelves, plates slip from the drain board, knives unhook from the walls. I touch the toaster and I get an electric shock. I make a pot of coffee and it tastes like poison. The kitchen wants to kill me! It's not nine in the A.M. yet, and already I have death on the brain. Do you know what that's like, Beth? Everywhere I turn, it's death! I can't get in my tub without thinking death — I think it's a coffin. Death, Beth! I take a shower and I think gas is going to come out. I'm taking sponge baths! Sponge baths over a basin! Why do you think I have my hair all pinned up like this? Because it's dirty! I can't bear to put my head under water!

BETHANY. Let me do something for you, Adel. Please let me! What can I do?

ADEL. You can — stop hugging my ankles! — You can ... you can brush my hair.

BETHANY. Yes! I can do that! Let me!

ADEL. *(Removing a brush from her bag.)* I can't stand it — my scalp's driving me crazy. *(Bethany kneels behind Adel's chair and begins removing her hairpins and brushing her hair.)*

BETHANY. Do you hate me, Adel?

ADEL. I wanted to die when Carl told me he was in love with you. I tried to end myself when he said you'd been ... sleeping together ... for so long. *(A knot in her hair.)* Ouch!

BETHANY. I'm sorry, Adel! I'm sorry!

ADEL. Christ, am I itchy!

BETHANY. Forgive me!

ADEL. I thought you were my friend, Beth!

BETHANY. I am, Adel, I am! I don't know what I was thinking of at the time.

ADEL. For four years? Ouch!

BETHANY. I'm sorry.

ADEL. I don't know what it was, but I didn't feel safe anymore. I started suspecting everything. My doctor — she's an idiot — she said, "Adel, don't ever kill yourself without first making your bed and doing all the dishes in the sink." Well, I *never* did those things to begin with. So I fired the maid. Now my bed's an unmade mess and I haven't a clean plate in the house and I'm *still* alive!

BETHANY. Adel, I don't love Carl. I don't love him. I don't think I *ever* loved him. I think I only loved the way my body moved beneath his. I think I was loving myself. I never thought of Carl. I'm not thinking of him now.

ADEL. Okay, now start styling it.

BETHANY. I never loved Carl. I only loved making love to him. I think I realized this when it no longer was a secret, when Carl told Alvin.

ADEL. Stop brushing and start styling!

BETHANY. You know, Adel, I've never had a orgasm with Alvin. Never. I don't even know if he knows it. Sometimes I think he's oblivious to everything. Living in a world of pots and pans.

ADEL. I asked Alvin if I could move in here because I can't stand living at home alone.

BETHANY. You don't want to move in here, Adel. You don't know what it's like to live with Alvin. Do you know what he does? He labels everything, puts little gummed stickers on everything with its name on it. As if he's going to forget everything in a minute.

ADEL. I hate living alone.

BETHANY. We have a girl come in on Fridays to vacuum — Alvin *helps* her!

ADEL. *(Picking up the silver tray and holding it up like a mirror.)* Oh, Beth. I like what you're doing!

BETHANY. Alvin is a terrible lover. He gives silly little chipmunk kisses.

ADEL. *(Holding up a hairpin.)* Here's another pin.

BETHANY. *(Standing up.)* You know what, Adel? We should go away together, go away and leave everything.

ADEL. Go away with you?

BETHANY. Yes! What do you need Carl for? Carl was no good for you anyway.

ADEL. No good for me?

BETHANY. He said you were completely unresponsive.

ADEL. Carl said this?

BETHANY. He said that you were squeamish.

ADEL. Carl told you this?

BETHANY. He said that he's always loved you, though.

ADEL. Carl said these things to you?

BETHANY. Carl is a trap! Let me massage your back. *(She gets up on the table, kneels, and massages Adel's neck, back, and shoulders.)*

ADEL. Carl once told me that I was boring in bed. That's what he says about Zoe in chapter twenty. I want him dead!

BETHANY. Where is your tension? Let me massage it.

ADEL. Carl used me!

BETHANY. Carl is a trap.

ADEL. Don't you think I know about traps, Beth? Seven years, and I appear *briefly* in the last chapter of a book which holds *no* interest past the middle — no matter *what* the national book people say!

BETHANY. How does this feel? Let me undo these buttons so I can really get in.

ADEL. I have something to learn about traps, Beth? A man — and I'm talking about Carl — who in bed called me every possible name —

79

Claudia! Valerie! Laura! Gaby! Zoe! Marsha! Barbara! Amy! Seven years, and never Adel! … "Open your eyes, Carl!" I'd shout, "open your eyes and see *who you are fucking*! — I'm not a Zoe or an Amy, I'm an Adel!" Now you, Beth — and I never blamed you — want to tell me about traps? If my mother had lived to see my trap coming, she would have killed herself and then me!

BETHANY. Is this working, Adel?

ADEL. You want to know who's *really* boring? Carl and his love novels! And I am *sick* of that love shit. She loves him, he loves her, you love them, they love you — love shit! *(Taking a gulp of what is left of a glass of wine. Wincing.)* What year is this? It's so bitter!

BETHANY. I feel my poetry returning to me.

ADEL. That's good. Harder. Easy. Easy. Good. Real good. I'm coming back to life. "Forgive and relax," my doctor says. Advice at her rates I don't need. She can go to hell! I'm writing an exposé novel on *Carl*. You hear me, Beth? I will reveal each of his cruelties in detail — it'll have to be published in volumes.

BETHANY. Good, Adel!

ADEL. Want to collaborate?

BETHANY. I must return to poetry. Carl has stunted my muse. To write I must dip into my well of pain. How deep it is! Carl has no well and therefore must dip into ours. That's why he's always hanging over us. Although he doesn't seem to need us, he does. He sits waiting to dip in.

ADEL. I know the well of pain, Beth! I know it. I keep choking, and I don't know what to do. Every night is the same as the last. Spiders crawl up onto my bedspread and tell me I'm no good. They talk to me, Beth! They tell me I'm worthless and should go die. It's not a nightmare — it's my life.

BETHANY. Life is a torture chamber, Adel. I thought of that while crawling home. Ten men stopped me and offered to put me in a taxi, and I said no! Let me crawl home, maybe then I'll miss a few of the flying knives that come out each day to attack us.

ADEL. Those are the knives from my kitchen!

BETHANY. I'm returning to poetry, Adel. I'm turning my back on love. I'm turning to the cauldron of art. My muse is back!

> *Betrayal weighs on me like so much fake jewelry,*
> *Seized by a gloved hand,*
> *It falls like so many unstrung beads on a tiled floor …*

Look how the lines are coming to me, Adel!

*Love is the rack I have been tied to,*
*A machine of delicate tortures.*
*My heart on fire seizes the whip I once cracked under ...*
Adel, listen!
*And pushes me, pushes me ...*
*(She stands on the table.)* Adel, the floor is turning! Do you feel it!
Under our feet. *(She loses her balance for a moment.)* The earth *twists*
under our shoes, Adel!
*I am the master of my ...*
*(Losing her balance again.)* Adel, hold me! The floor is turning! I can't
stand up! *(Adel gets on the table with Bethany. They support one another.)*
ADEL.  Beth, did you say that Carl has always loved me? He said
that? That he's always loved me?
BETHANY.  *(Back to poetry.)*
*Betrayal! Betrayal! And vengeance: The perfume of history.*
*The noxious scent of coupling ...*
Coupling what, Adel? Help me.
*So many lovers falling away like rows of ... rows of ...*
ADEL.  Valium. Rows of Valium?
BETHANY.
*Like so many rows of Valium,*
*The tiny tombstones of the spirit.*
ADEL.  I like that.
BETHANY.
*What is love but torture?*
*The thumbscrews of the heart tightening,*
*Gripping the half-hopes —*
ADEL.  Carl thinks *he* can write!
BETHANY.
*— And chokers of disappointment,*
*The brooch of promises,*
*That stickpin of the breast*
*And the mismatched earrings of marriage:*
*The culprit on top of it.*
*What is love?*
ADEL.  Torture!
BETHANY.
*Again: What is love?*
ADEL and BETHANY.
*Torture!*

ADEL. *(A tiny voice.)* But I still love Carl.

BETHANY.
> *And men: what are men?*

Tell it, Adel!

ADEL. Torture!

BETHANY. Again!

ADEL and BETHANY.
> *Torture!*

ADEL. *(A tiny voice.)* But I still love Carl.

BETHANY.
> *The weak men and the strong men!*
> *Together they are dust.*
> *So much dust soiling*
> *The apparel of women.*
> *So much filth emerging*
> *From the misguided wombs*
> *Of their unhappy mothers.*
> *What is life?*
> *What is life, Adel?!*

ADEL and BETHANY.
> *Torture!*

*(Enter Carl.)*

ADEL. Carl!

BETHANY. Vengeance!

CARL. Beth, I'm sorry. I guess I made a lot of phone calls. I got carried away by my award.

BETHANY. DON'T EVEN TOUCH ME!

CARL. I guess we're a finished chapter.

BETHANY. *(Throwing a box of chocolates at Carl.)* Eat shit!

CARL. The affair is over, that's obvious. Hello, Adel.

ADEL. I came here to kill you, Carl.

CARL. No, you didn't.

ADEL. Yes, I did. Didn't I, Beth?

BETHANY. Don't trust him — he's a rat with a necktie!

ADEL. *(Uncertain of her path.)* I'm going to kill you, Carl.

CARL. You're not going to kill me or anyone else. You couldn't even kill yourself, Adel.

ADEL. He's trying to pull out my stitches! You see!

CARL. Who took you to the hospital, Adel, and sat with you for ten hours until they said you could go home? Who signed the papers of responsibility, so you wouldn't have to spend the night in the hospital?

ADEL. My doctor.

CARL. No, Adel. Your doctor was the one who said she wanted to discontinue treatment because your progress was too slow.

ADEL. No!

CARL. I'm the one who persuaded her to keep you on.

ADEL. You did?

BETHANY. LIES!

CARL. Has Beth told you about the award?

ADEL. *(Taking out the letter.)* I have the letter.

CARL. And you came here to deliver it to me. How sweet of you, Adel. And in two weeks, Adel, we'll be able to go to the award banquet, and you'll sit next to me. Maybe you'll be all healed by then. Then we could forget all this. Wouldn't that be nice?

ADEL. Home with you?

BETHANY. And be killed, Adel? Save yourself!

ADEL. I'm writing an exposé on you, Carl. An exposé for the world to read.

CARL. I'll help you with it.

ADEL. You won't be very popular after it's published, Carl. You'll be banned in libraries.

CARL. That's good.

BETHANY. The table's moving!

CARL. I have the dogs back. I've gotten Prince and King out of the kennel, and they want to see you.

ADEL. Prince and King are back?

BETHANY. Adel!

ADEL. Beth says you don't love me!

CARL. I do.

BETHANY. What are you saying, Adel?!

ADEL. Beth says you don't want me.

CARL. I do.

BETHANY. Stop it! Everything is getting twisted!

CARL. What's twisted, Beth? Explain it.

BETHANY. You think I'm Georgette. Georgette, chapters seven through eleven.

ADEL. Eight through eleven.

BETHANY. We're just characters in your goddamned plagiarized books! Adel — you're Zoe, Zoe in chapter twenty. Shoplifting lingerie in expensive stores. Adel, let us spit on him!

CARL. Bethany, apparently some demon has taken residence in you.

BETHANY. *(Throwing down a plate.)* I won't be a character in a book!

CARL. Try to get some facts straight. A) My books are fiction. B) The critics have awarded my book —

ADEL. I typed it, Carl.

CARL. — *The Motel of the Heart* — the *best* piece of fiction of the year, and C) Any similarities to *life* are coincidental.

ADEL. A, B, C.

BETHANY. BULLSHIT! Crawling through the gutter while you were on the telephone, I realized something: I am not a victim in a novel, I'm a poet! *(Grabbing a flower from the centerpiece.)* I WON'T WEAR LOST LOVE LIKE A CORSAGE …

CARL. You're really gone, Beth, aren't you?

BETHANY. I'm a better writer than you are, Carl. We're all better than you are! You're a *bad* novelist, a *bad* man!

CARL. A poet! How long are you going to go on sending the same five poems to *The New Yorker*, Beth? You think they're amnesiacs?

BETHANY. *(Spitting out each word.)* I HOPE YOUR BOOKS DON'T SELL!

CARL. Why don't you shut up?

BETHANY. You think you're God! A little miniature God — a fraud! *(Enter Alvin.)*

ALVIN. I had a visitation.

ADEL and CARL. Alvin!

ALVIN. I had a visitation. On Park Avenue. I saw God.

BETHANY. Alvin, I don't love you anymore. I don't know what love is. I hate love.

ALVIN. Beth, you're back.

CARL. Alvin, Adel and I are getting back together.

ADEL. What?

ALVIN. I saw God standing in a kind of kitchen.

ADEL. On Park Avenue?

ALVIN. It was indescribable. Sharp knives and forks, a huge cutting board, all kinds of vegetables.

CARL. Alvin, are you all right?

ALVIN. Everything's in season. There's no frozen food. It's like paradise.

ADEL. What did he say, Alvin? What did God say?

ALVIN. He didn't say anything.

ADEL. Nothing?

ALVIN. God doesn't say anything because he knows all the recipes by heart.

BETHANY. I'm dizzy. Dizzy and sick.

ADEL. You mean you didn't ask him anything?

ALVIN. I didn't, Adel. I didn't ask him anything. I was ashamed. I don't know why, but I was ashamed.

BETHANY. I feel the table moving. Slowly. In a circle.

CARL. She's back on that kick again.

ALVIN. Look at all the broken things.

ADEL. Carl, the apartment wants to kill me. I can't bathe. I can't eat. I can't go in the kitchen.

BETHANY. Let's go away, Adel — we'll eat out all the time — we don't need them!

ALVIN. Are you in love with Adel?

CARL. Let's go home, Adel, come on.

ADEL. Home with you?

CARL. Come on, Adel.

ALVIN. You know that I love you, Beth. I love you still.

BETHANY. *(Pushing things off the sides of the table.)* Enough! I've had enough!

CARL. Come on, Adel, I have a taxi waiting outside.

ADEL. What should I do, Beth?

BETHANY. Adel, don't go.

ALVIN. I know now that things are not what they seemed.

BETHANY. They're even worse than that, Alvin, they stink!

CARL. *(Picking Adel up like a bride.)* Adel's coming with me.

BETHANY. Adel!

ADEL. *(Pleading.)* Beth, I don't want to be alone, I'm afraid. I don't want to be alone, forgive me. I don't want to be alone, I can't.

ALVIN. Something is happening to us. We are being punished.

BETHANY. The floor is moving!

CARL. That's because the earth is moving. It's turning on its axis. *(Moving toward the door.)* We're going now.

BETHANY. The floor is moving!

ALVIN. Oh, God, say something. I'm so unhappy.

## End of Play

# PROPERTY LIST

Dirty plates, cutlery
Half-filled wine glasses
Unfolded napkins
Unlit candles
Floral centerpiece with removable flower
Pots, pans
Sponges, dishwashing soap
Decanter of wine
Cake on platter
Box of chocolates
Locket/pillbox with Valium
Handbag
Lipstick
Valium container
Award letter
Small packet of notes
Silver tray, bowl of water, washcloth, soap
Hairbrush
Hairpins

# A SINGULAR
# KINDA GUY

## BY DAVID IVES

# CHARACTERS

MITCH

# A SINGULAR KINDA GUY

*Lights up on Mitch, a guy out on a Saturday night.*

MITCH. I know what you're thinking. You're looking at me and you're saying to yourself, "Average guy. Normal human being. Nothing out of the ordinary." Well, that's what I thought too, for lots of years, and boy, was I wrong. Now I look back, I think I always really knew the truth about myself, underneath. It's like, sometimes I'd look in the mirror in the morning and I'd get this weird feeling like what I was looking at was not what I really was looking at. Or else I'd be standing in a crowd of people at a party, and suddenly I'd get this idea like I was standing in a huge empty space and there wasn't anybody around me for miles. Episodes of "vastation," if you know that beautiful word. And then one day I had a ... I don't know what you'd call it. A mystical experience?

I was walking down Lex over in the Thirties when I go by this old office supply shop. A crummy little place, kinda dusty. But I turn and I look and I see ... in the window ... an Olivetti model 250 portable electric typewriter. Are you familiar with that particular model? Have you ever seen the old Olivetti 250? Well, let me tell you — it is sublime. The lines. The shape. The slant of the keyboard. It's all there! It's a thing of beauty!

Anyway, I'm standing there looking at this thing, and it's like I recognize it from someplace. It's like I'm looking at family somehow, like I'm seeing some long-lost older brother for the first time, and suddenly I realize — *that's me*, right there. That thing in the window is exactly what I feel like, on the inside. Same lines, same shape, same aesthetic. And what I realized was — I am a typewriter. No, really! A typewriter! All those years I thought I was a human being, on the inside I was really a portable Olivetti 250 with automatic correctability. And you know what? I can't even type!

Needless to say, this revelation came as a shock. But all of a sudden it's clear to me how come I always got off on big words — like "vastation." Or "phenomenological." Or "subcutaneous." Words are what a typewriter's all about, right?

Problem is, it can be a lonely thing, being a typewriter in a world of human beings. And now here I am, totally replaced by computers. Who needs a typewriter anymore? Here I finally figure out what I really am — I'm an antique already!

Plus, there's my love life, which is problematical to say the least. The difficulties involved in a typewriter finding a suitable partner in this town are fairly prodigious, as you can imagine. At least now I know how come I always loved ... not just sex, sex is anywhere, but ... touch. Being touched, and touching. Being touched is part of the nature and purpose of typewriters, that's how we express ourselves and the human person along with us. Hands on the keyboard and the right touch — fire away. Yeah, women's hands. They're practically the first thing I notice. Nice set of shapely fingers. Good manicure. No hangnails. Soft skin. I'm not a finger fetishist or anything, you understand, it's just ...

You've got a pretty nice pair of hands there yourself. That's what I noticed, that's how come I stepped over here to talk to you. I know all this sounds pretty loony, but you know I've never told anybody this before? Somehow I just felt like I could trust you, and ...

What? I beg your pardon?

I don't understand.

You're not really a girl? Sure, you're a girl, you're a beautiful girl, so ...

You're what? You're actually a sheet of paper? French ten-pound bond? Ivory-tinted? Pure Egyptian cotton fiber ... with the watermark of a heron? *(Holds out his hand.)* Glad to meet you. *(Blackout.)*

## End of Play

# SOMETHING FROM NOTHING

## BY DAVID RIEDY

## CHARACTERS

ROY — 40, your average Joe,
probably wears a Yankees cap.

NINA — 30, dressed for a party.

SKIP — 30, dressed for a party (less successfully).

## SETTING

The A train at night.

SOMETHING FROM NOTHING was first produced by Atrain
Productions (Lawrence Feeney, Executive Producer) as part of
theAtrainplays, Vol. 8, at the Neighborhood Playhouse in New York
City, in November 2003. It was directed by Gregory Simmons. The
cast was as follows:

ROY ....................................................................... Rob Sheridan
NINA ....................................................................... Nancy Wu
SKIP ....................................................................... Scott Wood

# SOMETHING FROM NOTHING

*Roy stands and looks out at the audience. Nina sits on the bench, clutching a large shopping bag, looking off into the middle distance.*

ROY. That's the thing about subways. You can never tell — well, sometimes you can, but most of the time it's just — You don't know. The person sitting next to you could — well, probably not. Well, most likely not. I mean how likely is it that someone at random could change — *(Looks at Nina. Turns back to the audience.)* I'm not the kind of person to do — what I did. *(Crosses back to Nina to sit next to her.)* On the A train, somewhere near 96th street on that long patch of dark tunnel heading south into what I call The City Proper, I looked down from the Bronx Zoo ads and saw a leg. *(Looks down at Nina's leg.)* And for a moment it seemed okay — it seemed like it would be all right — of course not, but it seemed like it would be acceptable for me to touch it, with the kind of casualness you'd have with a lover, or — a lover. *(Beat.)* And then — I touched it. *(Puts his hand casually on Nina's knee. Nina looks at him, aghast. They lock eyes. Nina leaps up.)*
NINA. What the hell are you doing?
ROY. What?
NINA. What the fuck do you think you are doing? *(To empty seat next to where she was sitting.)* He touched my leg!
ROY. I'm sorry. Did I? I'm really —
NINA. You can't do that!
ROY. I know!
NINA. That is incorrect behavior! *(To empty seat.)* Isn't it, Skip?!
ROY. I know, and I apologize —

NINA. No apology will be accepted! That was a breach of human-interaction etiquette and, as such, is punishable by the strongest amount of shame that I can muster.

ROY. *(To audience.)* Or something like that.

NINA. You are a bad man!

ROY. *(To audience.)* And then the boyfriend said ... Oh. There was a boyfriend. *(Skip appears onstage.)*

SKIP. ... And furthermore, my position as the aggrieved partner in this heterosexual couple requires me to threaten you with force, violence, bodily harm if you do not show the appropriate amount of remorse and slink away in the corner or get off at the next stop.

ROY. *(To audience.)* I pointed out that the next stop was ten minutes away. *(Skip chases Roy.)*

SKIP. Remorse! I want to see remorse!

ROY. Remorse! I have great remorse!

NINA. *(Stopping Skip from attacking Roy.)* Don't hurt him!

SKIP. Remorse!

ROY. Remorse!

NINA. I'm beginning to have feelings of pity ...

SKIP. No pity!

NINA. Pity. *(Skip goes after Roy again.)*

SKIP. Remorse!

ROY. Remorse! *(Nina puts herself between the two of them.)*

NINA. He seems to be a gentle person who would never hurt —

ROY. I wouldn't, no —

NINA. Never hurt anyone.

ROY. I'm an ant!

SKIP. Ants don't feel remorse.

ROY. I'm an ant stuck on this giant — well, bigger than giant, unfathomably huge — ball of dirt teeming with life. One of billions — trillions of organisms scratching and climbing the hills of the world, trying to find my way — to find a path — and in front of me for a moment there seemed — there wasn't, I know — but there seemed to be an opportunity to ... share, or enjoy — Not, you know ... enjoy — but to reach out and not be alone, and to touch another ant ...

SKIP. *(To audience.)* And that's when I hit him. *(Roy falls onto the bench as if punched. Skip and Nina sit quietly on the bench; Nina holds her bag again, as at the top of the play.)* But from the beginning he had it coming and he knew he had it coming. We're on the train heading home from a party in Washington Heights that she didn't want to go to because it was my friends and people she didn't know. She'd been quiet all evening — as if something was bothering her — in her unobtrusive, no-I'm-not-suffering-don't-mind-me-have-a-good-time-I'll-be-fine way. *(Sits next to Nina. To Nina.)* You okay?

NINA. I'm fine.

SKIP. *(Looks to the audience as if to say, "See?" To audience.)* And yet, I was feeling these intense — swells of love. As if my heart was growing or a new fountain of appreciation had sprung up inside of me and was making exotic water patterns to a new song of adoration. And I reached over to take her hand so I could squeeze it in a long-term-casual, deeply-loving-but-minor-gesture kind of way, and this guy — this nondescript everyman, think-I've-seen-him-before-somewhere-but-probably-not kind of guy reaches over and squeezes her knee in an I-belong-here-just-as-much-as-the-next-guy kind of way! And she just sat there, looking at him. And he's looking at her — and I couldn't take it anymore — *(To Roy.)* What the hell are you doing?

ROY. What?

SKIP. What do you mean what?

ROY. I was just —

NINA. Skip.

SKIP. No — what's going on here?

ROY. I don't know what you're — ?

NINA. Skip, relax.

SKIP. Did he just touch your leg?

NINA. Yes.

SKIP. And you're okay with that?

ROY. I'm sorry about that.

NINA. He was just —

ROY. I was just —

SKIP. WHAT?

ROY. I was just feeling very lonely.

SKIP. I want to hear from her.

NINA. Hear what?

SKIP. Are you okay with random guys touching your knee?

NINA. No.

SKIP. Do you know this guy?

NINA. No.

SKIP. Did he touch your knee?

NINA. Yes.

SKIP. So he's a random guy touching your knee!

NINA. Yes?

SKIP. And you're okay with that?

NINA. Not usually!

ROY. Let me explain ...

SKIP. *(To audience.)* And — okay — so this is where I yelled at the guy a little bit and maybe pushed him around and threatened him. But I didn't hit him. Not at first. *(Sits next to Nina. To Nina.)* What's going on with you?

NINA. Nothing.

SKIP. Something's going on with you, and something's not nothing.

NINA. Don't make something out of nothing.

SKIP. The entire time at Ken's you hid in the bedroom.

NINA. I did not.

SKIP. Reading some book — what were you reading? *(Tries to grab Nina's bag. Nina stops him.)*

NINA. Nothing.

SKIP. C'mon — I'm a sensitive guy. I'm a caring boyfriend. You talk to me. We talk about your mother. We talk about your foot problems ... about your menstruation.

NINA. There's nothing to talk about.

SKIP. You could tell me.

NINA. I would tell you if there was something to tell.

SKIP. Really?

NINA. Yes.

SKIP. *(To audience.)* I really am a caring guy, in a non-ironic, I-really-do-care-about-other-people's-feelings kind of way. *(To Nina.)* I worry about you. About us.

NINA. Don't.

SKIP. Don't worry?

NINA. Don't say that.

SKIP. But ... I'm communicating.

NINA. Sometimes you talk about nothing and you turn it into something. Just let it go. Let me go.

SKIP. "Let me go"? *(Nina turns away. Roy approaches Skip. To audience.)* And that's when the guy came up and —

ROY. You are an insignificant ant. A blight on this earth. Unable to find your way. She is a beautiful butterfly whose love you will never earn —

SKIP. *(To audience.)* And that's when I hit him. *(Roy falls onto the bench as if punched. Nina holds her bag. Skip sits next to her in tableau.)*
NINA. *(To audience.)* I was remembering that feeling of lying on top of the water wearing nothing but a bikini, fins, and a snorkel mask and not moving. Watching the reef twenty feet below me. All the fishes darting in and out. Brightly colored fish — black-nosed, blue-finned, a red comb on top. How peaceful it was. Just the sounds of your own breath, the buzzing of salt in your ears — as if you're not there anymore. I'd stay there for hours if I could. If Skip would let me. But he would swim up and make grunting noises and point at something I was already looking at — and then I'd be back in my body again, and I'd feel heavy. We'd been at this party — some kind of going away or welcome home — Skip's friends — but I knew one of them. Skip didn't know, but I'd had an affair with one of them — Ken. It was more of a combustion than an affair. I couldn't look at Ken. My skin felt hot, and steam seemed to rise from my arms and face. So I hid, or tried to. I found myself in Ken's bedroom. And — after only fifteen minutes of searching — I came across his journals. I wanted to know why we stopped — why we started — why him? When we left, I threw all his journals into my bag, next to the casserole dish. On the train home I wanted to read them, but I didn't want to hurt Skip. What am I, crazy? I loved Skip. Really. And then this guy touched my leg. *(Roy briefly touches Nina's leg and looks away.)* Did you just touch my leg?
ROY. I think I did. I'm sorry.
NINA. Why did you — ?
ROY. I don't know.
NINA. It scared me.
ROY. I'm sorry. It was really weird of me to do that.
SKIP. What's going on?
NINA. Nothing.
SKIP. Okay.
NINA. Do you know me?
ROY. No.
NINA. Why would you do that?
ROY. I'm lonely.
NINA. So you touch other people's legs?
ROY. No! I'm not some random guy who touches other people's legs!
NINA. But you touched mine.

ROY. I did.

NINA. Did I — look like I would like you to touch my leg?

SKIP. Are you sure you're — ?

NINA. Everything's fine.

SKIP. Okay. Good.

NINA. This man just touched my leg.

SKIP. HE WHAT??! *(Leaps up, ready for action.)*

NINA. *(To audience.)* And that's when Skip got angry. *(To Skip.)* It's okay.

SKIP. He touched your leg!

NINA. It's okay. I didn't mind.

SKIP. Of course you minded! He tried to rape you!

NINA. No!

SKIP. I will defend your honor! *(Chases after Roy. They do a lap around the car.)*

NINA. And that's when the fight started! Skip chased him around the car. The guy tried to escape to the next car, but Skip followed him. *(Roy exits to another car, and Skip follows.)* The guy climbed outside the cars, and Skip followed! *(Roy, pursued by Skip, leaps out and grabs hold of the outside of the subway car. Roy and Skip shimmy down the side of the car, Skip trying to pull Roy off. Roy starts prying the doors open on one end of the car, and Skip follows suit on the other doors.)* I shouted, "Stop! Stop!" a couple of times, but Skip didn't hear me. I love Skip, but he tends to overreact. *(The doors open, and Roy and Skip fall inside the subway. Skip lurches to his feet and begins to chase Roy.)* I know he was trying to defend me. I know he was showing me he loves me, but sometimes I wish he'd just leave me alone! *(The chase stops, frozen.)* So I could float. *(Beat.)*

ROY. I'm an ant! *(Skip cocks his arm back.)*

NINA. And then Skip punched him. *(A slow-motion punch. She watches Skip, unimpressed. Roy falls onto the bench.)* Skip! *(Back to real time, she goes to Roy.)*

SKIP. What?!

NINA. *(To Roy.)* Are you all right?

SKIP. Don't help him up! I just knocked him down!

ROY. I'm okay.

NINA. You don't need to go hitting everyone!

SKIP. I don't hit everyone.

NINA. *(Helping Roy.)* Here —

SKIP. He's fine.

ROY. I'm okay.

SKIP. I mean, I hit him really hard, but he'll be fine.

ROY. I'm sorry I touched your leg.

NINA. It's okay.

ROY. I didn't mean anything by it.

NINA. I know. I could tell.

SKIP. Nina. Get away from him.

NINA. You shouldn't have hit him. He wasn't threatening you or me.

ROY. Is your hand okay?

SKIP. It's fine. It's nothing. *(To audience.)* And I felt like when I was a kid, reading a grown-up book, and the hero makes a choice that is good or noble or wise but that — to my thirteen-year-old self seemed wrong — in an I-don't-really-understand-people-at-all, is-something-wrong-with-me kind of way. And I realized that I don't. I don't know what's in her bag. I don't know why he touched her leg, or why she was okay with it. And I don't know why I shouldn't have hit him. *(Beat.)*

ROY. *(To audience.)* And then they left.

NINA. *(To audience.)* We got off at the next stop.

SKIP. *(To audience.)* I went left, and she went right.

ROY. *(To audience.)* And it was like nothing had happened.

SKIP. *(To audience.)* That was the last time I saw her.

ROY. *(To audience.)* But something must have happened.

NINA. *(To audience.)* I took the journals home, although I never did read them.

ROY. *(To audience.)* That's the thing about subways: sometimes — not always, but sometimes — the person next to you — You become the kind of person who does the kind of things you wouldn't do. Sometimes a stranger can change — well, but probably not.

**End of Play**

# PROPERTY LIST

Large shopping bag

# THERE'S NO
# HERE HERE

## BY CRAIG POSPISIL

# CHARACTERS

JULIETTE — beautiful and chic.

A STRANGER — an older woman in frumpy clothes,
who we will come to learn is named Gertrude.

A WAITER — a bored French waiter,
who we will come to learn is named Jean-Luc.

LANCE — an American writer.

# SETTING

A Parisian café. Spring.

*For Lanford Wilson.*

THERE'S NO HERE HERE had its professional premiere at Barrington Stage Company (Julianne Boyd, Artistic Director; Triston Wilson, Managing Director) in Pittsfield, Massachusetts, as part of the 10x10 Upstreet Arts Festival in February 2013. It was directed by Christopher Innvar. The cast was as follows:

JULIETTE ...................................................... Emily Taplin Boyd
STRANGER ................................................ Peggy Pharr Wilson
WAITER........................................................ Scott Drummond
LANCE ............................................................ Dustin Charles

# THERE'S NO HERE HERE

*A Parisian café. Spring. French music, perhaps something by Serge Gainsbourg, plays in the background.\**

*Juliette sits at a small table, reading Camus' L'Étranger. A menu lies on the table. An older woman in frumpy clothes sits at another table with her back to the audience. She does not turn around until indicated. She has a glass of rosé wine, which she sips from time to time.*

*A bored French waiter in a white apron enters with a cup of coffee, which he sets down on Juliette's table. She nods a thank-you to him. He gestures to the menu on her table to ask, "Anything else?" Juliette shakes her head, "No." The waiter shrugs, a little put out, but it means less work for him. He takes the menu and starts to exit, when Lance comes barreling in, carrying a notebook.*

*Juliette looks up as Lance stops in front of her.*

LANCE.  You can't touch someone's life like that and then just be done with them! *(Juliette stares at Lance, confused. She looks at the waiter, who shrugs. They both look at Lance, who drops his notebook on Juliette's table and turns to the audience.)* At least, that's what I wanted to say. *(Slight pause.)* There's a lot of things I want to say. I don't actually say most of them. *(Slight pause.)* Or anything like them really. It comes out wrong. *(Slight pause.)* So, that's what I wanted to say, but I think what I actually said was: *(Turning back to Juliette, plaintively.)* Why won't you answer my calls?
JULIETTE.  *Lance … Chérie, cette chose entre nous, c'est fini.*

---

\* See Special Note on Songs and Recordings on copyright page.

LANCE. *(Winces and holds up his hand to Juliette to say, "Wait." Turns back to the audience.)* Sorry. Uh, we're in France. Paris, actually. Left Bank, not far from the Seine. Does everyone speak French? No? *(Turning back to the others.)* You've got to speak in English.

JULIETTE. *Quoi?*

LANCE. *Parlez en anglais.*

JULIETTE. *Pourquoi?*

LANCE. *Parce que. (Points at the audience. Juliette sighs and shrugs.)*

JULIETTE. Okay. *(Lance looks at the waiter, who shakes his head.)*

WAITER. *Non.*

LANCE. Come on.

WAITER. *Non.*

LANCE. They won't understand. That's rude.

WAITER. *Oui. (Exits. Lance turns back to Juliette, who goes back to her book.)*

LANCE. Juliette —

JULIETTE. I have nothing to say to you.

LANCE. You're being unreasonable.

JULIETTE. I am a French woman.

LANCE. But this is why I'm here. I came here to write.

JULIETTE. Oh, yes, you saved, for years you saved so you could come to Paris and write, just to write.

LANCE. Yes! But now there's also you.

JULIETTE. Hmmmpf. *(Continues reading. Lance reaches over and takes the book from her hands.)*

LANCE. Juliette —

JULIETTE. *Donnez-moi mon livre!*

LANCE. In English.

JULIETTE. Give me my book! *(Lance hands her back the book.)* You want to write, fine. Go be with your words. I have words too, and my words are "Good-bye."

LANCE. All I said was that I needed to work this afternoon.

JULIETTE. Yes, one afternoon after another. Hmmmpf.

LANCE. Why can't we just talk about this?

JULIETTE. You talk and you talk and you talk until the talking is over.

STRANGER. *(Turning around.)* Oh, I like that. *(Lance and Juliette look at her.)* Don't mind me, I'm just listening in.

LANCE. Um … we're having a private conversation.

STRANGER. In a public place.

LANCE. Do you mind?

STRANGER. All right. I'm sorry.

LANCE. That's okay.

STRANGER. You don't mean that.

LANCE. Sure, I do.

STRANGER. No, you're just being polite.

JULIETTE. Who is this person?

LANCE. I have no idea.

STRANGER. Yes, you do.

LANCE. No. I don't.

STRANGER. You're never going to write something true if you keep that up. *(Lance stops and stares at her. On some level he recognizes her, but he's unable to place her.)*

LANCE. Wait, are ... who are you?

STRANGER. *Garçon? (The waiter, full of ennui, enters.)*

WAITER. *Oui, madame?*

STRANGER. A glass of rosé, please.

WAITER. *Certainement. (Exits.)*

LANCE. You already have a glass of wine.

STRANGER. It won't last forever.

JULIETTE. Ooo! You come here, you interrupt my reading, saying you must talk to me, why won't I talk to you ... and then you stand and talk with this ... stranger. Meanwhile my café crème has gone cold and my temper is hot.

STRANGER. She's a spitfire.

LANCE. Just hold on, there's something ...

JULIETTE. There is something, yes, there is something! This is how it always is with you. You see only what is right in front of you and the rest just fades away. You expect me — me, a beautiful French woman! — to be here when you want me, but even when you are here, you are not here.

STRANGER. There's no here here. *(The waiter returns with a glass of wine, which he sets on her table.)*

WAITER. *Voilà, madame.*

STRANGER. *Merci. (The waiter turns and leaves again. She swirls the wine in her glass and takes a sniff of its bouquet.)* A rosé is a rosé is a rosé.

LANCE. Oh, my god!

JULIETTE. What?

LANCE.  She's Gertrude Stein!

JULIETTE.  Who?

LANCE.  A famous American writer who lived in Paris in the 1920s and '30s.

JULIETTE.  That's impossible.

GERTRUDE.  I prefer it that way. If it can be done, why do it?

LANCE.  No, no, no … *(Turning to the audience.)* I'm sorry, I don't know why she's here. *(Back to Gertrude.)* You can't be here. You're dead. *(Back to the audience.)* She's dead.

GERTRUDE.  Who are you talking to?

LANCE.  Them.

GERTRUDE.  So, having a fight with your girlfriend in café in Paris while an audience somewhere else watches you is okay, but talking to a woman who's been dead since 1946, *that's* going too far?

LANCE.  Okay, this is … this is …

GERTRUDE.  This is your story.

LANCE.  Story?

JULIETTE.  Wait, you are writing this?

LANCE.  Oh, my god, I think I am.

JULIETTE.  You! You come to make this big scene here at the café, to talk, to make me take you back … but you are somewhere *still* writing?!

LANCE.  *(A beat.)* Yes?

JULIETTE.  You are a bad writer.

LANCE.  Juliette, you —

JULIETTE.  *(Cutting him off.)* And! You are a bad lover.

GERTRUDE.  Bam, said the lady.

LANCE.  Do you mind?!

GERTRUDE.  Hey, this is your imagination. You don't want me here, say the word.

LANCE.  Go!

GERTRUDE.  That's not the word.

LANCE.  Look, please just … go back to your table and finish your wine.

GERTRUDE.  Sorry, Lance. I aim to misbehave. *(Hearing wine mentioned, the waiter returns.)*

WAITER.  *Un peu plus de vin?*

LANCE.  Juliette, please, this is —

JULIETTE.  Don't bother speaking. I hear the lies already.

LANCE. No. I'm here to write. This could be my last chance. Something either happens this year or ... I've been doing this since I was twenty-two, and all I've got to show are a couple of short stories in an anthology, an agent that won't take my calls, and ... I'm divorced. I don't have any kids. I have a cat. I found her in an alley around the corner from here, and I call her Elle. I saved her life, but she only pays attention to me when it's time to eat. I just want to get something down on the page that's alive. But I haven't been able to. Then I met you, and I feel something. And it inspires me to write, and — *(Juliette slaps him.)*
GERTRUDE. Affection can be so dangerous.
WAITER. *Pardon, monsieur, mais —*
LANCE. Would you go away? Can't you just ignore us like most Parisian waiters?!
WAITER. No. I will not. I have, as you say, a bone to pick. My role in this story of yours is nothing more than an insulting cliché. A rude French waiter? *Oo-la-la!* So clever. How ever did you come up with an idea such as that? Feh! No wonder you have no success. You have the imagination of a cow. I don't even have a name in this scenario of yours. *(Waving a hand toward the audience.)* To them, I am just the French waiter, full of ennui, saying only *"oui"* and *"non"* because your French is too poor to allow me to truly give voice to all that is inside me. And I am supposed to just go in and out, bringing you wine and coffee while you play out this ridiculous scene with this woman, telling her you "feel something," instead of telling her you love her. If you love her, you take action. You don't plead and moan about writing words. What are words? Will they love you anymore than your cat? But like all Americans, all you think of is yourself, and you miss the point completely. In love, you should act, and act decisively! A woman like this needs to be grabbed hard, and then held tenderly. *(Suddenly takes hold of Juliette's arms, pulls her to him in a flash, and then instantly holds her tenderly in his arms. Their faces are close. He caresses her face with one hand.)* Darling. Your cool beauty overwhelms me. You are like a tonic to a man lying in bed with malaria and a high fever, on the knife's edge between life and death. You are water in the desert. You give me life, you give me breath.
JULIETTE. Oh, Jean-Luc.
JEAN-LUC. *(Suavely.)* Yes ... *(Looking to Lance.)* That is my name.
JULIETTE. Jean-Luc, will you take me away from here?

JEAN-LUC.  Yes, my darling. We'll leave this behind, start anew. Come with me to the casbah.

JULIETTE.  Yes, yes, I will. If we go now we can still catch the night plane. *(She and Jean-Luc kiss passionately. When they break apart, Jean-Luc turns dismissively to Lance.)*

JEAN-LUC.  That is how you keep a woman like Juliette.

JULIETTE.  *Oui, c'est vrai. (Looks out at the audience, remembering to speak in English.)* I mean —

LANCE.  No, it's okay. I think they get it. *(Juliette kisses Lance on both cheeks.)*

JULIETTE.  *Au revoir, chéri.*

LANCE.  *Au revoir. (Jean-Luc takes off his apron, drops it on the ground, and takes Juliette's hand. They hurry offstage. Lance watches them go.)*

GERTRUDE.  That's what happens when you ignore minor characters. They come back and bite you in the ass.

LANCE.  I'm starting to wonder who the minor character here really is.

GERTRUDE.  You don't understand what you don't understand.

LANCE.  What?

GERTRUDE.  Think about it.

LANCE.  *(Pause.)* I'm blind to the parts of myself that I don't want to hear.

GERTRUDE.  Oh, I like that.

LANCE.  Yeah. *(Sits down at the table and begins to write in his notebook. Gertrude gets the glass of rosé from her table and sets it down by him.)*

GERTRUDE.  To write is to write is to write is to write … but you might get thirsty along the way. *(Lance continues to write. She smiles and gently pats the back of Lance's head, caressing his hair lightly.)* Good man, Lance. You keep working. *(Turns and makes her way off down the boulevard as the lights fade on Lance, who keeps writing.)*

**End of Play**

# PROPERTY LIST

Menu
Book
Glass of rosé
Cup of coffee
Notebook
Pen

# SOUND EFFECTS

Music

# YOU HAVE ARRIVED

## BY ROB ACKERMAN

# CHARACTERS

DAN, in his 20s.

KRISTIN, in her 20s.

CYNDI, up to you.

# SETTING

New York City. Night. A car (two chairs side by side).

YOU HAVE ARRIVED was first performed as part of Pop, a benefit for At Hand Theatre Company (Dan Horrigan, Artistic Director) at the Algonquin Theatre in New York City in 2008. It was directd by Rebecca A. Hengstenberg. The cast was as follows:

DAN ........................................................................ Jake Paque
KRISTIN ..................................................... Colleen B. McGloin
CYNDI ..................................................... Lea McKenna-Garcia

# YOU HAVE ARRIVED

*Dan sits in the driver's seat and peers out, looking for someone. On a low stool in front of him, to his right, sits Cyndi, a GPS navigator. Her head is at the height of the imaginary dashboard, and her eyes are fixed forward in concentration. She has two chimes in her lap, and right now she rings them: bing-bong.*

CYNDI.  "You have arrived." *(Dan speaks to the back of her head. Throughout the play, she's determined to remain impassive, a machine.)*
DAN.  Fuck. Where is she? I don't know why I even try.
KRISTIN.  *(Steps out of the shadows.)* Dan?
DAN.  Oh. Hey. Kristin.
KRISTIN.  Hey. *(Dan climbs out, kisses her cheeks, helps her in.)*
DAN.  Gosh, I couldn't see you over there.
KRISTIN.  I told you I'd be here. Red scarf. Converse sneakers.
DAN.  Yeah, you did.
KRISTIN.  And you found me, Dan. Way to go.
DAN.  Well, I didn't. She did. *(Points to Cyndi.)*
KRISTIN.  She?
DAN.  My navigator.
KRISTIN.  Oh, wow, look at that.
DAN.  I always get lost in all these tiny streets — Stanton, Rivington, Ludlow — but she knows where to go.
KRISTIN.  "She's" a computer.
DAN.  No, she's not. She's a receiver, a transponder, a cartographic data display device with calibrated voice prompts. She's a navigator, a global positioning system is what she is, really.
KRISTIN.  A computer, Dan.
DAN.  Yeah, I guess.
KRISTIN.  A computer is not a person. You can't personify.
DAN.  *(Nervous.)* Oh, I loved that in high school. No. I guess it was actually seventh grade. Mister Trowbridge. He made us learn all

those words. Words of literature. Made us feel all scholarly and philosophical and poetical. I remember all the words. Personification. Alliteration. Irony. (Irony was the best. I loved irony. "The laughter of the gods.") Oh, and euphony ... and metonymy.

KRISTIN. Metonymy?

DAN. That's when one thing stands for something else. Like if you say, "Damn, that BMW just rear-ended me!" It didn't actually rear-end *you*, it rear-ended your old Subaru Outback, you know?

KRISTIN. Does your navigator stand for you, Dan?

DAN. No. She's a she. I'm a he. *(Through the following, he focuses his attention on the back of Cyndi's head and uses his index finger to enter commands.)*

CYNDI. Main menu.

KRISTIN. Oh, I like her voice.

CYNDI. Enter address.

KRISTIN. Wow. She's got a great voice. Does she have a name?

DAN. Cyndi. Yeah. She's Cyndi.

KRISTIN. I like that. Do you really call her Cyndi?

DAN. I do now.

KRISTIN. Is she easy to use?

CYNDI. My addresses.

DAN. Like an iPhone, kinda — you play with her touchscreen and tell her what to do.

KRISTIN. "Hey, Cyndi. I'm on a blind date. Take me to Williamsburg."

DAN. Basically.

CYNDI. Previous destinations.

DAN. A lot of times I have go to work at five in the morning and hunt for some house in Far Rockaway, and a Mapquest printout just doesn't cut it, so I'm like, "If these things ever go below two hundred bucks, I'm getting one."

CYNDI. Route.

KRISTIN. And she was...?

DAN. One ninety-nine ninety-nine. They're even cheaper now, of course, and they've got better ones that tell you what street you're turning on to and stuff, but she's all right. I mean, she gets the job done.

CYNDI. Calculating route.

DAN. *(Starts driving.)* So how long have you known Tim?

KRISTIN. I dated him, in high school.

DAN. Was it serious?

KRISTIN. It kinda was.

DAN.  He told me you were cute. *(Beat.)* You are cute.

CYNDI.  Left turn in point-two miles.

KRISTIN.  Thanks, I guess.

DAN.  So you're a "graphic designer"?

KRISTIN.  Well, sort of. I know Photoshop and HTML. I do a lot of temp work.

DAN.  Join the club. Isn't it weird how there are some things in school that are totally useful, and others that are such total crap you're like, "Why do they even bother?" You know, like word problems.

CYNDI.  Make a left.

DAN.  Fuck. Shit. Sorry.

KRISTIN.  No, that's okay.

DAN.  Where was I? *(Turns the wheel sharply, and Kristin flinches.)*

KRISTIN.  Word problems.

DAN.  Oh. Yeah. Okay, word problems are like, "If Jack is meeting Sally and it's rush hour, then what time should Jack depart?" But who cares? Jack can call Sally's cell and say he's running late. She's probably got an issue of *The New Yorker* in her purse — she can deal with sitting there and having a Frappuccino. You can't expect Jack to start crunching a bunch of numbers. I mean, Jesus. Math is fucked.

KRISTIN.  And metonymy is useful?

CYNDI.  Left turn in point-two miles.

DAN.  Sure, Cyndi, whatever you say.

KRISTIN.  *(Studies the GPS screen.)* I like how she shows us where we are. We're this little arrow, just moving along. There's the river. You can see the bridge.

CYNDI.  Make a left. *(Dan turns carefully. She rings her chimes.)*

DAN.  The background is black because it's nighttime. In the daytime the screen is all green and blue, and if there's a golf course anywhere in the vicinity, she always lets you know. Whoever made this thing is really big on golf courses and country clubs.

CYNDI.  Remain on the current road for one mile.

KRISTIN.  Oh-kay.

DAN.  Yeah, it always weirds me out when she says that. Makes me want to make a quick turn just to tick her off, see how she reacts. But she won't react, she'll just say, "Calculating route." That's how she copes with human frailty.

KRISTIN.  "Calculating route."

DAN.  Anything goes wrong, she never gets angry, never loses patience, just says …

KRISTIN. "Calculating route."

CYNDI. Remain on the current road. *(Rings her chimes again.)*

DAN. Her chimes mean we've hit some sort of satellite coordinate, I think. But she doesn't always ring her chimes. You can't count on it. Sometimes she does, sometimes she doesn't. She's a little loopy like that.

CYNDI. Keep to the right in one mile.

KRISTIN. You know, people used to do just fine before they had these things. Ernest Shackleton saved a whole stranded expedition in Antarctica with nothing but a compass and a sextant.

DAN. Good for him.

KRISTIN. I majored in math with a concentration in geography.

DAN. So I guess you like word problems?

KRISTIN. I love them.

CYNDI. Keep to the right.

DAN. I am keeping to the right, bitch.

KRISTIN. Don't talk to her like that.

DAN. She's a machine.

KRISTIN. No, she's Cyndi.

DAN. Look, I don't have a sextant like Shackleton. And I can't even find my way around Brooklyn, much less Antarctica. I always end up in Greenpoint, circling that stinky sewage-treatment plant, and that's not the best way to start a date.

KRISTIN. Neither is being insulting to women, Dan.

DAN. Cyndi is not a woman.

KRISTIN. She sounds like a woman.

CYNDI. Right turn in point-two miles.

KRISTIN. Take Kent Street.

DAN. *(Raises a hand.)* Wait for Cyndi.

CYNDI. Make a right. *(Rings her chimes, and Dan turns.)*

KRISTIN. You trust a machine over me — what's your problem?

DAN. You know, it's hard being a guy sometimes. First girls get taller and get boobs and all we get is zits, then they turn out to be smarter and more mature, and they're too cool to call us back or call each other bitches.

KRISTIN. We call each other bitches, we just don't like it when cute guys call us bitches.

DAN. Am I a cute guy?

KRISTIN. Lemme get back to you on that.

CYNDI. Right turn in point-three miles.

DAN. Thank you, Cyndi.

KRISTIN. Good. That's better. *(A quiet moment, and then ... )*

DAN. I'm sorry about your cat. Tim told me. Mushroom.

KRISTIN. He was great. He was twelve. I had him since sixth grade.

DAN. I'm really sorry.

KRISTIN. Thanks. *(They both breathe.)*

DAN. There's one thing Cyndi says.

CYNDI. Make a right turn.

DAN. One thing I really like.

KRISTIN. What?

DAN. You'll see. She'll say it when we get there. *(Beat.)* It's one of those phrases that means more than it means.

KRISTIN. Irony?

DAN. Yeah. It's positively fraught with irony. The good kind.

KRISTIN. She better not call anybody a bitch.

CYNDI. Approaching destination on the right.

KRISTIN. You know what you've got, Dan? You've got this weird resentment. You rush to judgment on the basis of stuff that's not there, like, I don't know, like ghosts of girlfriends past or something.

DAN. I don't know what you're talking about.

KRISTIN. Look, I'm on this date with you, and I kinda hate you, but Tim said you're a good guy, so let's just try to make the best of it, okay? I'm just me. I just met you. And I'm not the girl who hurt your feelings.

DAN. Hurt my feelings?

KRISTIN. I'm hoping that's what happened. I'm hoping there's a real reason you're being such a jerk. We're both nervous. Are we gonna like each other, hate each other, hook up? That has yet to be detemined. But chill out. Having fun is more important. Having fun might possibly be the most important thing in the world, and almost everyone is pretty bad at it. Now, *that's* ironic.

DAN. Uh-huh.

KRISTIN. How do you feel about fun, Dan?

DAN. I, I'm okay with it.

KRISTIN. So am I.

DAN. Kristin ...

KRISTIN. Yeah.

DAN. Let's have fun.

CYNDI. *(Rings her chimes.)* You have arrived. *(Blackout.)*

## End of Play

117

# PROPERTY LIST

Two chairs
Chimes

# APPENDIX

# NEW PLAYS

★ **MOTHERS AND SONS by Terrence McNally.** At turns funny and powerful, MOTHERS AND SONS portrays a woman who pays an unexpected visit to the New York apartment of her late son's partner, who is now married to another man and has a young son. Challenged to face how society has changed around her, generations collide as she revisits the past and begins to see the life her son might have led. "A resonant elegy for a ravaged generation." –NY Times. "A moving reflection on a changed America." –Chicago Tribune. [2M, 1W, 1 boy] ISBN: 978-0-8222-3183-7

★ **THE HEIR APPARENT by David Ives, adapted from Le Légataire Universel by Jean-François Regnard.** Paris, 1708. Eraste, a worthy though penniless young man, is in love with the fair Isabelle, but her forbidding mother, Madame Argante, will only let the two marry if Eraste can show he will inherit the estate of his rich but miserly Uncle Geronte. Unfortunately, old Geronte has also fallen for the fair Isabelle, and plans to marry her this very day and leave her everything in his will—separating the two young lovers forever. Eraste's wily servant Crispin jumps in, getting a couple of meddling relatives disinherited by impersonating them (one, a brash American, the other a French female country cousin)—only to have the old man kick off before his will is made! In a brilliant stroke, Crispin then impersonates the old man, dictating a will favorable to his master (and Crispin himself, of course)—only to find that rich Uncle Geronte isn't dead at all and is more than ever ready to marry Isabelle! The multiple strands of the plot are unraveled to great comic effect in the streaming rhyming couplets of French classical comedy, and everyone lives happily, and richly, ever after. [4M, 3W] ISBN: 978-0-8222-2808-0

★ **HANDLE WITH CARE by Jason Odell Williams.** Circumstances both hilarious and tragic bring together a young Israeli woman, who has little command of English, and a young American man, who has little command of romance. Is their inevitable love an accident…or is it destiny, generations in the making? "A hilarious and heartwarming romantic comedy." –NY Times. "Hilariously funny! Utterly charming, fearlessly adorable and a tiny bit magical." –Naples News. [2M, 2W] ISBN: 978-0-8222-3138-7

★ **LAST GAS by John Cariani.** Nat Paradis is a Red Sox-loving part-time dad who manages Paradis' Last Convenient Store, the last convenient place to get gas—or anything—before the Canadian border to the north and the North Maine Woods to the west. When an old flame returns to town, Nat gets a chance to rekindle a romance he gave up on years ago. But sparks fly as he's forced to choose between new love and old. "Peppered with poignant characters [and] sharp writing." –Portland Phoenix. "Very funny and surprisingly thought-provoking." –Portland Press Herald. [4M, 3W] ISBN: 978-0-8222-3232-2

**DRAMATISTS PLAY SERVICE, INC.**
**440 Park Avenue South, New York, NY 10016  212-683-8960  Fax 212-213-1539**
**postmaster@dramatists.com   www.dramatists.com**

# NEW PLAYS

★ **ACT ONE by James Lapine.** Growing up in an impoverished Bronx family and forced to drop out of school at age thirteen, Moss Hart dreamed of joining the glamorous world of the theater. Hart's famous memoir *Act One* plots his unlikely collaboration with the legendary playwright George S. Kaufman and his arrival on Broadway. Tony Award-winning writer and director James Lapine has adapted Act One for the stage, creating a funny, heartbreaking and suspenseful celebration of a playwright and his work. "…brims contagiously with the ineffable, irrational and irrefutable passion for that endangered religion called the Theater." –NY Times. "…wrought with abundant skill and empathy." –Time Out. [8M, 4W] ISBN: 978-0-8222-3217-9

★ **THE VEIL by Conor McPherson.** May 1822, rural Ireland. The defrocked Reverend Berkeley arrives at the crumbling former glory of Mount Prospect House to accompany a young woman to England. Seventeen-year-old Hannah is to be married off to a marquis in order to resolve the debts of her mother's estate. However, compelled by the strange voices that haunt his beautiful young charge and a fascination with the psychic current that pervades the house, Berkeley proposes a séance, the consequences of which are catastrophic. "…an effective mixture of dark comedy and suspense." –Telegraph (London). "A cracking fireside tale of haunting and decay." –Times (London). [3M, 5W] ISBN: 978-0-8222-3313-8

★ **AN OCTOROON by Branden Jacobs-Jenkins. Winner of the 2014 OBIE Award for Best New American Play.** Judge Peyton is dead and his plantation Terrebonne is in financial ruins. Peyton's handsome nephew George arrives as heir apparent and quickly falls in love with Zoe, a beautiful octoroon. But the evil overseer M'Closky has other plans—for both Terrebonne and Zoe. In 1859, a famous Irishman wrote this play about slavery in America. Now an American tries to write his own. "AN OCTOROON invites us to laugh loudly and easily at how naïve the old stereotypes now seem, until nothing seems funny at all." –NY Times [10M, 5W] ISBN: 978-0-8222-3226-1

★ **IVANOV translated and adapted by Curt Columbus.** In this fascinating early work by Anton Chekhov, we see the union of humor and pathos that would become his trademark. A restless man, Nicholai Ivanov struggles to dig himself out of debt and out of provincial boredom. When the local doctor, Lvov, informs Ivanov that his wife Anna is dying and accuses him of worsening her condition with his foul moods, Ivanov is sent into a downward spiral of depression and ennui. He soon finds himself drawn to a beautiful young woman, Sasha, full of hope and energy. Finding himself stuck between a romantic young mistress and his ailing wife, Ivanov falls deeper into crisis, heading toward inevitable tragedy. [8M, 8W] ISBN: 978-0-8222-3155-4

**DRAMATISTS PLAY SERVICE, INC.**
**440 Park Avenue South, New York, NY 10016  212-683-8960  Fax 212-213-1539**
**postmaster@dramatists.com  www.dramatists.com**

# NEW PLAYS

★ **I'LL EAT YOU LAST: A CHAT WITH SUE MENGERS by John Logan.** For more than 20 years, Sue Mengers' clients were the biggest names in show business: Barbra Streisand, Faye Dunaway, Burt Reynolds, Ali MacGraw, Gene Hackman, Cher, Candice Bergen, Ryan O'Neal, Nick Nolte, Mike Nichols, Gore Vidal, Bob Fosse…If her clients were the talk of the town, she was the town, and her dinner parties were the envy of Hollywood. Now, you're invited into her glamorous Beverly Hills home for an evening of dish, dirty secrets and all the inside showbiz details only Sue can tell you. "A delectable soufflé of a solo show…thanks to the buoyant, witty writing of Mr. Logan" –NY Times. "80 irresistible minutes of primo tinseltown dish from a certified master chef." –Hollywood Reporter. [1W] ISBN: 978-0-8222-3079-3

★ **PUNK ROCK by Simon Stephens.** In a private school outside of Manchester, England, a group of highly-articulate seventeen-year-olds flirt and posture their way through the day while preparing for their A-Level mock exams. With hormones raging and minimal adult supervision, the students must prepare for their future — and survive the savagery of high school. Inspired by playwright Simon Stephens' own experiences as a teacher, PUNK ROCK is an honest and unnerving chronicle of contemporary adolescence. "[A] tender, ferocious and frightning play." –NY Times. "[A] muscular little play that starts out funny and ferocious then reveals its compassion by degrees." –Hollywood Reporter. [5M, 3W] ISBN: 978-0-8222-3288-9

★ **THE COUNTRY HOUSE by Donald Margulies.** A brood of famous and longing-to-be-famous creative artists have gathered at their summer home during the Williamstown Theatre Festival. When the weekend takes an unexpected turn, everyone is forced to improvise, inciting a series of simmering jealousies, romantic outbursts, and passionate soul-searching. Both witty and compelling, THE COUNTRY HOUSE provides a piercing look at a family of performers coming to terms with the roles they play in each other's lives. "A valentine to the artists of the stage." –NY Times. "Remarkably candid and funny." –Variety. [3M, 3W] ISBN: 978-0-8222-3274-2

★ **OUR LADY OF KIBEHO by Katori Hall.** Based on real events, OUR LADY OF KIBEHO is an exploration of faith, doubt, and the power and consequences of both. In 1981, a village girl in Rwanda claims to see the Virgin Mary. Ostracized by her schoolmates and labeled disturbed, everyone refuses to believe, until impossible happenings appear again and again. Skepticism gives way to fear, and then to belief, causing upheaval in the school community and beyond. "Transfixing." –NY Times. "Hall's passionate play renews belief in what theater can do." –Time Out [7M, 8W, 1 boy] ISBN: 978-0-8222-3301-5

**DRAMATISTS PLAY SERVICE, INC.**
**440 Park Avenue South, New York, NY 10016  212-683-8960  Fax 212-213-1539**
**postmaster@dramatists.com  www.dramatists.com**

# NEW PLAYS

★ **AGES OF THE MOON by Sam Shepard.** Byron and Ames are old friends, reunited by mutual desperation. Over bourbon on ice, they sit, reflect and bicker until fifty years of love, friendship and rivalry are put to the test at the barrel of a gun. "A poignant and honest continuation of themes that have always been present in the work of one of this country's most important dramatists, here reconsidered in the light and shadow of time passed." –NY Times. "Finely wrought...as enjoyable and enlightening as a night spent stargazing." –Talkin' Broadway. [2M] ISBN: 978-0-8222-2462-4

★ **ALL THE WAY by Robert Schenkkan. Winner of the 2014 Tony Award for Best Play.** November, 1963. An assassin's bullet catapults Lyndon Baines Johnson into the presidency. A Shakespearean figure of towering ambition and appetite, this charismatic, conflicted Texan hurls himself into the passage of the Civil Rights Act—a tinderbox issue emblematic of a divided America—even as he campaigns for re-election in his own right, and the recognition he so desperately wants. In Pulitzer Prize and Tony Award–winning Robert Schenkkan's vivid dramatization of LBJ's first year in office, means versus ends plays out on the precipice of modern America. ALL THE WAY is a searing, enthralling exploration of the morality of power. It's not personal, it's just politics. "...action-packed, thoroughly gripping... jaw-dropping political drama." –Variety. "A theatrical coup...nonstop action. The suspense of a first-class thriller." –NY1. [17M, 3W] ISBN: 978-0-8222-3181-3

★ **CHOIR BOY by Tarell Alvin McCraney.** The Charles R. Drew Prep School for Boys is dedicated to the creation of strong, ethical black men. Pharus wants nothing more than to take his rightful place as leader of the school's legendary gospel choir. Can he find his way inside the hallowed halls of this institution if he sings in his own key? "[An] affecting and honest portrait...of a gay youth tentatively beginning to find the courage to let the truth about himself become known." –NY Times. "In his stirring and stylishly told drama, Tarell Alvin McCraney cannily explores race and sexuality and the graces and gravity of history." –NY Daily News. [7M] ISBN: 978-0-8222-3116-5

★ **THE ELECTRIC BABY by Stefanie Zadravec.** When Helen causes a car accident that kills a young man, a group of fractured souls cross paths and connect around a mysterious dying baby who glows like the moon. Folk tales and folklore weave throughout this magical story of sad endings, strange beginnings and the unlikely people that get you from one place to the next. "The imperceptible magic that pervades human existence and the power of myth to assuage sorrow are invoked by the playwright as she entwines the lives of strangers in THE ELECTRIC BABY, a touching drama." –NY Times. "As dazzling as the dialogue is dreamful." –Pittsburgh City Paper. [3M, 3W] ISBN: 978-0-8222-3011-3

**DRAMATISTS PLAY SERVICE, INC.**
**440 Park Avenue South, New York, NY 10016  212-683-8960  Fax 212-213-1539**
**postmaster@dramatists.com  www.dramatists.com**